101 Movement Games
for Children

Other Smart Fun Books:

101 Music Games for Children by Jerry Storms

101 Dance Games for Children by Paul Rooyackers

101 Drama Games for Children by Paul Rooyackers

101 More Music Games for Children by Jerry Storms

Ordering

Trade bookstores in the U.S. and Canada, please contact:

Publishers Group West
1700 Fourth Street, Berkeley CA 94710
Phone: (800) 788-3123 Fax: (510) 528-3444

Hunter House books are available at bulk discounts for course adoptions;
to qualifying community, health care, and government organizations;
and for special promotions and fund-raising. For details please contact:

Special Sales Department
Hunter House Inc., PO Box 2914, Alameda CA 94501-0914
Phone: (510) 865-5282 Fax: (510) 865-4295
E-mail: ordering@hunterhouse.com

Individuals can order our books from most bookstores,
by calling toll-free **(800) 266-5592**, or from our
website at **www.hunterhouse.com**

101
Movement Games

Children

Fun and Learning with Playful Moving

Huberta Wiertsema

Translated by Amina Marix Evans &
Illustrated by Cecilia Bowman & Astrid Sibbes

a Hunter House $Smart Fun$ book

First published in the Netherlands in 1991 by Panta Rhei as
Honderd Bewegingsspelen

Hunter House Inc., Publishers
PO Box 2914
Alameda CA 94501-0914

Library of Congress Cataloging-in-Publication Data
Wiertsema, Huberta.

[Honderd bewegingsspelen. English]
101 movement games for children ; fun and learning with playful moving
/ Huberta Wiertsma.— 1st ed.

p. cm. — (A Hunter House smartfun book)
Includes index.
ISBN 0-89793-346-X (pb) — ISBN 0-89793-347-8 (sp)
1. Games. 2. Movement education. I. Title: One hundred one movement
games for children. II. Title: One hundred and one movement games for children.
III. Title. IV. Series.
GV1203 .W672 2001
371.33 7—dc21   2001039423

Project Credits

Cover Design and Book Production:
   Jil Weil

Book Design: Hunter House

Developmental and Copy Editor:
   Ashley Chase

Proofreader: John David Marion

Acquisitions Editor: Jeanne Brondino

Associate Editor: Alexandra Mummery

Publicity Manager: Sara Long

Sales and Marketing Assistant:
   Earlita K. Chenault

Customer Service Manager:
   Christina Sverdrup

Order Fulfillment: Lakdhon Lama

Administrator: Theresa Nelson

Computer Support: Peter Eichelberger

Publisher: Kiran S. Rana

Printed by Bang Printing, Brainerd, Minnesota

Manufactured in the United States of America

9 8 7 6 5 4 3 2 1   First Edition   02 03 04 05 06

Contents

*A detailed list of the games indicating
appropriate age groups begins on the next page.*

List of Games

List of Games, continued

Preface

In this book you will find more than one hundred movement games, an even greater number of variations on the games, and practical hints for leading the games. These games focus on pure movement, rather than dance or music. Some of the games are based on old playground games, others on children's games from around the globe, and still others on drama exercises.

Movement games can be used in schools, camps, workshops, and many other contexts. Within the field of education, they are particularly applicable to physical education, dance, and drama.

We have chosen games based on the following criteria: The games must be fun, they must not require a great deal of experience, and they must contribute to the personal, social, or creative growth of the participants.

These games can be used by almost anyone. Most are simple to learn. The only requirements are a belief in the value of the game and a capacity to enjoy movement and play.

I would like to dedicate this work to the children, teenagers, and adults with whom I have worked. Without their cooperation, humor, and criticism, this book would not exist. I hope that the reader will derive as much pleasure from the games as we have.

Good luck!

Huberta Wiertsema
The Netherlands

For easy reading we have alternated use of the male and female pronouns. Of course, every "he" also means "she," and vice versa!

Introduction

Play

Play is special. In a make-believe situation, our imagination has free reign. In games we are invited to take risks that would be very unwise in real life. We might pretend we are hunting a dragon that can kill with the mere touch of one of its heads. When we see the creature, we don't run away, even though flight would be the most natural reaction. We step bravely forward. In the game, eternal life is a reality. If we are tagged, nothing has really happened. We can be revived to join in the next attack.

By engaging in make-believe, by surrendering to the game and to our imaginations, we release new powers. We may gain fresh insight, self-confidence, or energy. These renewed powers can help us to deal with daily reality better. This is the value and the attraction of play.

Movement

Movement is essential for human beings. We must move our bodies to keep them healthy. More importantly, it is movement that allows us to discover and make contact with other people, our surroundings, and even ourselves.

The way in which you move tells something about who you are. Your body language is an expression of what moves you emotionally, what you believe, and what interests you. Your body is your instrument, your means of expression.

Playful Movement

The central theme of this book is playful movement. The starting point is spontaneous play. Children play in order to understand life. Movement games allow us to learn by doing.

In movement games, players must think about using their bodies as a means of expression. This is the real value of the movement games—they connect thought, feeling, and action. Moving playfully engages the whole person, body and soul.

Objectives

Movement games can be used to help develop players' personal, social, and creative skills. The following pages cover these areas of development.

Personal Development

Movement games can be used to good effect as a means of personal development. The games foster personal development in the following areas:

- **improving sensory awareness**
  Many games require players to sharpen their senses. They may have to listen or look to find their fellow players. In other games, players might be asked to close their eyes and think about how it feels to make a particular movement. In this way, players learn to focus on one sense at a time.

- **improving ease and skill of movement**
  Some games concentrate on developing hand-eye coordination, while others are directed toward agility, flexibility, quick reactions, physical expressiveness, or the consciousness of one's own body.

- **improving orientation in the surroundings**
  In movement games, the use of the space plays an important role. Players learn to orient themselves within the space. They must consider: How large is the space? How can they use it? What is their relationship to the space?

- **increasing self-confidence and daring**
  In the games, players are challenged to take risks. They must react to new situations. Players' knowledge of and trust in their own capabilities increase through play.

Social Skills

The movement games are played in groups and are therefore extremely suitable for practicing social behavior. This book includes some competitive games. In these games, there is an element of achievement, but not at the expense of others. The achievement lies in this challenge to all the players: Make sure everyone has a good time! The games develop players' social skills in the following areas:

- **the experience of a group feeling**
  Many of the games are designed to increase a group's coherence. The participants quickly feel connected with each other, and this strengthens mutual communication. Players learn to be open to other peoples' ideas, consider each other, and work together to make the game fun.

- **trusting others**
  Groups who have worked together for a time may move on to trust games. These games challenge players to place their trust in other members of the group. This trust goes deeper than a feeling of comfort. The point is that players dare to trust others and dare to take responsibility for others who trust them.

- **expressing themselves in a group situation**
  Some games present the opportunity to be delightfully absorbed in the group. Players are not seen as individuals but as a collective. That gives security. This phase can be used effectively within the group process, but the process should not stop here. (For more on the group process, see pages 12–14.) The fundamental point is that individuals dare to show themselves with respect to the group, and that they know how to take responsibility for themselves. Many movement games are very well suited to this: for example, the expression games encourage players to show something of themselves, and the trust games promote responsibility. (See pages 102–115 and 94–101.)

- **working with and valuing differences**
  Diversity in a group can be a valuable resource, or a source of conflict. Some groups do not accept open difference: "Behave normally (and do exactly what we do), and you can be one of

us." These games offer opportunities to recognize the richness in the differences between people, to use these differences, and to value them.

Creative Skills

Because of their playful nature, movement games can used as a means of developing creative skills in the following areas:

- **using movement as a means of expression**
  Through play, the participants discover that their bodies can be instruments and develop their skills of physical expression. They do not simply exercise; they use movement to express a particular feeling or thought to other people.

  These expressions work both inwardly and outwardly: They put players in touch with themselves and with other people. Movement games tell the players something about themselves. Intentionally using the body to communicate helps participants recognize the unconscious messages they broadcast constantly with body language.

- **development of creativity, originality, and improvisation skills**
  Almost all movement games help develop creativity. Players engage in make-believe play in many games, and in others they improvise on a theme or a movement instruction. The games present challenges to which players must seek solutions outside the normal parameters. In these games, creative thought is directly linked to creative action.

The Role of the Leader

The leader's role involves more than simply explaining the game or keeping the score. The way in which the leader selects, introduces, and guides the games will greatly influence their effect on the participants.

Choosing a Game

As leader, one of your most important jobs is choosing the right game for the situation. Bear in mind the following points:

- **the group**

  What kind of group are you working with? How large is the group? How old are the participants? How much experience do the members of the group have, both with each other and in the area of play and movement? What is the atmosphere of the group? Try to put yourself in the players' position. Imagine what it will mean for that specific group to play that particular game. Is the game appropriate for the group? Are certain rules necessary to make it more interesting? Do you have to prepare the space? (See Suitability in terms of age, pages 6–7, and The size of the group needed, page 8.)

- **the objective**

  What are your aims in using a movement game? Will you use it as an icebreaker, as a warm up, or as a relaxation exercise? Do you want to put the emphasis on the individual, the relationships among the players, or the group as a whole? Formulate modest, clear, and attainable goals. In this way, you can lay the foundations for what you hope to achieve with the group.

- **the space**

  The space has a direct influence on the choice of game. Take note of the advantages and drawbacks of the space. How large is it? What are the acoustics like? What about the furnishings? Is the floor clean and free from splinters? Watch out for possible dangers such as sharp edges, columns, or a slippery floor. (See Amount of space needed, page 8.)

- **the time frame, time of day, and season**

  When choosing the games, consider: How much time will you have? At what time of day will you will be playing? Take the time of year and the weather into account as well. (See How long the game takes, page 7.)

- **your own preferences**

  Choose a game that suits you. If you like a particular game and are curious as to how it will work with the group, then you are already halfway there. You will infect the group with your enthusiasm. This does not mean that you need to try out every game yourself before leading the group, though it would be an advantage.

In short, in choosing a game, try to imagine the situation as fully as possible: the group, the time of day, the space. In this way, you will develop a feeling for the interaction of these factors. When in doubt, always select several games. You might choose one game to use if a particular group is rowdy and another in case the group turns out to be quiet.

How the Movement Games Are Organized

The games are grouped according to their objectives or their style of play. Each has been placed in the category on which the focus lies for the majority of players. The dividing lines are less strict than may appear at first glance. A concentration game may, for instance, also make a good cooperation game. In general, this is mentioned in the description of the game.

In the introduction to each type of game, the most important characteristics and effects of that kind of game are mentioned. As leader, familiarize yourself with the rules of each game before you try to explain it to the group. You may also want to keep the book handy as a reference.

The descriptions of most of the games include a number of suggested variations. I have pointed out any variations that work best for one particular age group.

Key to the Icons Used with the Games

To help you find games suitable for a particular situation, all the games are coded with symbols or icons. These icons tell you at a glance some things about the game:

- the appropriate grade level/age group
- the amount of time needed
- the size of the group needed
- the props required
- the space required

These are explained in more detail below.

Suitability in terms of age In determining the appropriate age group for each game, we have considered both the degree of difficulty and the interest level—for example: Is the game too complicated for younger players? Would older players consider the game's content childish? As leader, you might decide to change the rules according to the age of the players. The age groups correspond to grade level divisions commonly used in the educational system:

 = Young children in kindergarten through grade 2 (ages 4 through 8)

 = Older children in grades 3 through 5 (ages 8 through 11)

 = Adolescents in middle school, grades 6 through 8 (ages 11 through 14)

 = Teenagers in high school, grades 9 through 12 (ages 14 through 18)

 = All ages

How long the game takes The games are divided into those that require about 5 minutes, those that take 10 to 20 minutes, those that take 30 minutes, and those that take 40 minutes or more. The time indicated is the minimum time necessary to play each game successfully.

About 5 minutes

10 to 20 minutes

30 minutes

40 minutes or more

The size of the group needed While some games require an even number of players, multiples of threes, and so on, you can play many of the games with any sized group:

Amount of space needed Many movement games may be played in a small space, but a large space is ideal for most. If an appropriate space is not available, you might try adapting the game to suit the space. The games that require a large, gymnasium-sized space are marked with the following icon:

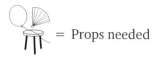 = Large space needed

Whether you need props Some games require the use of props, such as balls, boxes, or rope. These games are flagged with the following icon, and the necessary props are listed under the Materials heading:

 = Props needed

Musical accompaniment Several games include suggestions for suitable music. For instance, we might recommend either rhythmic or restful music.

Preparation

Prepare yourself mentally for what might happen as the group plays the game. Read through the game description carefully once. Try to visualize it: Watch it like a movie playing before your eyes. Think about the beginning phase. Consider what you are going to say and what rules you may have to introduce. Begin the game in your mind. Observe how it develops and picture what could go wrong. In your imagination, bring the game to a close and make the transition into the next activity. If you practice in the abstract, the reality is less likely to take you by surprise.

Some games require concrete preparation as well. Make sure that all necessary materials are available and ready.

Explaining the Game

Give a short, concise explanation so that the players will get into the game quickly. The players will want to see quick results, so give simple rules at the start and add more as the game progresses. Make sure that everyone can see you and that you can be heard. Speak clearly and use tone of voice to emphasize the most important points of the game.

Bring the game to life. Make sure that the players can see how it is developing. Put them in the starting position and give a clear example. Do it yourself, or let a few players demonstrate. With reaction or tag games it is fun to demonstrate in slow motion while you explain what will happen. Make sure participants learn the game through a combination of hearing, seeing, and doing.

Leading the Game

Stand in a position where you have a good view of the game. If play becomes dangerous or out of hand, stop the game immediately. In a positive manner, show the players where problems occurred and how play could be improved. During the game, give encouragement and instructions to the group or to individual players. Some types of games give the players a great deal of space for experimentation.

Sometimes during the game players discover possibilities you had not considered. For instance, in a game of tag, one child may find a place to hide and come out only when almost everyone has been caught. Show your surprise, praise the player for coming up with an original strategy, and discuss with the group whether or not this option may be used in the next round.

Sometimes you may decide to join in the game yourself. This will depend on the type of game, the group, and the purpose for which you are using the game. One major disadvantage is that you no longer have a complete view of how the game is going. In a game with opposing teams, you may risk drawing too much attention to yourself by joining one side. Young children in particular prefer to relate to a leader. One advantage of joining in the game is that it is easy to motivate the players. You also get hands-on experience of how the game works. Always choose a position from which you can guide the game effectively.

Below we give a few practical tips for the organization.

Organizing the Players

Ideally, everyone will join the game. Circumstances may prevent some members of the group from playing, however. In this case, organize the game so that everyone has a function. For example, you might appoint players to be umpires, scorekeepers, protectors in blindfold games, or deejays in charge of the cassette recorder.

Alternatively, you could give a special observation assignment to group members who must sit the game out. They might watch the players for examples of cooperation, use of space, clever tactics, and so on. Ask them to report back at the end.

Taking Turns

You can manage turn taking in the following ways:

- Pick someone yourself.
- Have the person who took the last turn pick someone (this involves friendship politics).
- Ask for volunteers and pick one.
- Think of a number, have players take guesses, and let the winner take the next turn.

As leader, you would be well advised to keep the choice in your own hands. It is quicker and you can ensure that everyone gets a turn.

Forming Groups

In general, groups of three to five players work best. There are various ways of forming these groups:

- Have players count off. For example, to form four groups, have players stand in a line and take turns calling out numbers in sequence from one to four. The number ones form a group, the number twos form another, and so on.

- Choose the groups yourself. In this case, nothing is left to chance.
- Make groups based on similarities, such as players' birth months or the initial letters of their names.
- Use a special game for forming groups. (See game number 44: "Group Seven" on page 72.)
- Leave it up to the players. For instance, ask them to make four groups of five people. Be aware that this method can create problems with children, since friends want to stay together and will only allow certain others into the group.

Working with Large Groups

Sometimes the group is larger than the optimal number of players for a particular game. Various solutions are possible:

- Split the group in half and have the two smaller groups work alongside each other. Use separate spaces or let the groups work in turn and watch each other. In this case, give the spectators an observation assignment. (See Organizing the Players, above.)
- Change the rules of the game so that it can be played with a larger group. For instance, have the players work in pairs.

Finishing the Game

Work up to a climax. You can bring the game to its climax by repeatedly challenging the players with new rules and variations. Players will get the hang of the game as they play and may begin to refine their strategy. When the game reaches its climax, all the players will be intensely involved. If you allow this phase to continue for too long, players will begin to drop out and the activity will lose its intensity. The best time to end the game is shortly after the climax. This calls for good observation. You must consider how the group and the individual players are involved in the game. Breaking off at this point ensures that players will be motivated for the next activity and that they will enjoy playing the game again the next time.

It is important to finish each game properly. This can be done in a number of ways depending on the type of game, the game's objective, and the makeup of the players. Here are some suggestions:

- Announce the score.
- Give your opinion about the way in which the group played the game.
- Ask the participants what they thought of the game. Be careful: An open question can lead anywhere. Phrase your question so that it relates to the aim of the game. For instance: "The object was to work together to hold the ball without using your hands. Did you manage to do that?" You might also have players say in turn what they did or experienced, or what parts of the game they found exciting, enjoyable, or annoying.
- Ask the players to evaluate the game or their own input. They can give ratings on a scale of one to five.
- Have the participants discuss in pairs or small groups what they found interesting about the game, or what they experienced.
- End the game in an active way. For instance, have players make a drawing about the game.

Setting Up a Games Program

In group work, these kinds of games do not stand in isolation but are part of a program. This program consists of a number of phases:

- introduction
- concentration
- exploration
- deepening
- closing

In this structure, you work step-by-step toward a particular goal.

Think about the ultimate objective of your work with the group. Will you focus on cooperation? Expression? Trust? Choose the game that best serves this goal. Although you chose it first, this is one of the last games the group will play. Now think about the skills players need in order to play that ultimate game well. Choose games for the earlier part of the program that will help players develop those skills. The modest objective of each successive game is to serve as a building block that helps lay the foundation for the larger goals of your work with the group. The phases of a typical program for group work using movement games are outlined below.

Introduction

The introductory phase puts players in the mood to move around and play. The introduction consists of a short activity in which the whole group is involved at the same time—for instance, a game of tag, a circle game, a song, a familiar children's game, or a discussion about the group's last gathering. (See Introduction Games, page 69 and Games of Tag, page 15.)

Concentration

Next, focus players' attention on the subject or theme central to the program. It is important to choose a game involving elements that will play a major role later on. For instance, if cooperation is the main theme, at this point you can use games such as number 14: "Where Are You?," page 30; number 16: "Mirror Game," page 33; or number 29: "Who Is the Leader?," page 49. (See also Concentration Games, page 29.)

Exploration

Concentration should move effortlessly into exploration. In this phase, the game should invite players to discover and experiment.

Players can explore individually or in small groups. The game will be intensive: Everyone will be working individually on the same activity, doing it in her own way. If the main emphasis of the program is on expression, exploration is an especially important phase. (See games number 21: "Freezing and Thawing," page 38; number 23: "Moving Joints," page 40; number 50: "Don't Drop the Ball," page 79; and number 86: "Roped In," page 125.)

Deepening

This is the crucial phase in which the group plays the game you chose first, around which you have planned the entire program. The previous phases were necessary to prepare players for this moment. In this phase, the group works most intensively toward your ultimate goal. For example, if your focus is on creativity, you might choose to play game number 69: "Group Storytelling," page 105; number 70: "Relay Story," page 106; or number 76: "Changing Statues," page 113.

Closing

Help the participants bring the activities to a satisfying close by discussing the games or presenting a movement piece or a short play. Sometimes it works well to end with a game that strengthens the group feeling, such as number 49: "In a Knot," page 77; number 52: "Headgear," page 82; or number 92: "The Atlas Game," page 134. Alternatively, you might have players sing a song with gestures.

Games of Tag

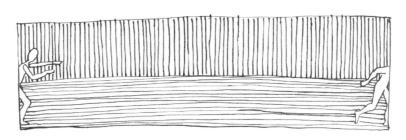

Tag games are pure movement games. It is great fun to chase after someone or to run away. Players must be alert. They watch out and react quickly. In a game of tag, players are sure to use every inch of available space. These games are perfectly suited as introductory games or as part of a warm-up. They are also perfect for blowing off steam.

Tag games are characterized by two roles: "It" (a player who chases) and runners who can be tagged. You can introduce many variations by adding different rules to these roles. For instance:

- Role reversal: The player who is tagged becomes "It."
- The one who is "It" can move only along a line marked on the ground (See game number 7: "Line Tag," page 22.)
- The players can move only in one particular way (for example, they must skip or hop on one foot).
- The players who have been tagged can be freed in some way.
- More than one person can be "It."

If you add new rules during the game, it will take on new dimensions and hold the players' interest.

A disadvantage of many tag games is that tagged players are removed from play. This can be easily avoided: The players who are out can come back into the game after a short time or they can play on in another area. They can also be freed by other players so that they can join the game again. In the descriptions of the games, these suggestions are developed further.

Lobster Soup

This exciting and strenuous tag game is well suited to a limited space: 10 x 7 yards is enough space for 16 players. Tell players that anyone who is tagged will turn into a "lobster." Demonstrate lobster position: Sit down on the floor with your knees bent and feet flat on the floor. Put your palms on the floor behind your back. Lift your bottom off the ground and "walk" on your hands and feet. Have players practice walking like lobsters. Then choose a player to be "It." Explain that "It" will begin the game running. As soon as he tags another player, both of them will turn into lobsters and try to tag the other players. Anyone who is tagged changes into a lobster and can also tag the others. Who will manage to remain standing in this teeming lobster soup?

Note: Players can only be tagged if they are touched with the hand. Lobsters have a tendency to strike out with their feet, but this can be dangerous. Any tags made this way do not count.

Code Tag

Tell players that anyone who is tagged in this game has to stand absolutely still, as if frozen. Explain that a player who is frozen can only be freed if another player performs a certain "code," or series of movements. You will find a few suggestions below. Have players agree on the code beforehand. After 2 minutes stop the game and count how many players are frozen. Then change the code, choose another player to be "It," and start the next 2-minute round. Possible codes:

- Touch the other player on both elbows, touch her knees, and touch her elbows again.
- Put your hand on the head of the player who is frozen and skip around her.
- Stand on one leg in front of the player, put your hands on her shoulders, and count to five aloud.

It is fun for the group to think up their own codes.

-counting by 5s, 2s, 10s

-EF hug, Spiderman hug, high 5, hug

-zoo-phonics   spell a word together

3

Liberation Tag

Tell players that this is a game of freeze tag: Anyone who is tagged has to freeze on the spot. Explain that one player, called the "liberator," can free frozen players by touching them. Choose someone to be "It" and have him close his eyes. Next, silently, choose a liberator. The liberator's identity must remain a secret from "It." Then let "It" open his eyes again and begin the game.

You might point out that "It" can gain an advantage by finding out who the liberator is. If he can tag this player, he will have free reign. It is in the group's best interest to keep the liberator's identity secret, and to protect her if necessary.

Will the player who is "It" manage to tag all the players within the time allowed? Does the group work well together to protect the liberator?

4

Cross-Tag

Explain to players that this tag game is unusual, because "It" chases after only one player at a time. At the start of the game, "It" will choose a target, call that player's name, and begin chasing her. Explain that if any player crosses the path between "It" and the target, that player becomes the new target. Point out that the target will change constantly. Tell students that the identity of "It" can change as well. If a player is tagged, she becomes the next "It." She should call out a name and try to tag that person.

Encourage players to think about how to use strategy in this game. The player who is being chased can run behind another player, making that player the new target. She can also ask for help from other players. The group members can try to save the target by getting between her and "It." In this way the game constantly takes new turns and can be very exciting.

I Dare You

Materials: chalk or masking tape for marking the ground

Use chalk or masking tape to mark three lines, one line down the center of the play space and two lines widely spaced on either side. The center line is the starting point, while the sidelines indicate the safe areas. Divide the group into pairs. Have partners stand on opposite sides of the starting line, facing each other. Tell the group that if a player touches his partner's hand, the partner can cross the center line to chase him. Explain that if the player reaches the safe area on his side before his partner can tag him, he wins a point. If he is tagged, his partner wins a point. Then they both return to the starting line. Encourage players to hold out their hands and dare each other to touch.

Choose new pairs after a few minutes and play the game again.

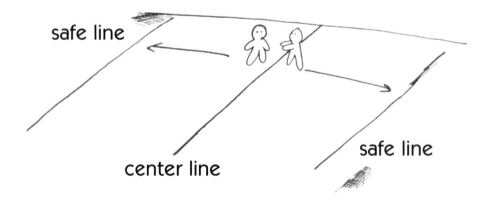

safe line

center line

safe line

6

Chase the Dragon's Tail

Tell players that this game originated in Asia, and versions of it are played in Vietnam, China, and Thailand, as well as many other countries.

Have players line up, with each player holding on to the hips or shoulders of the player in front of her. Explain that the first player in line is the head of the dragon, while the last player is the dragon's tail. Invite the head to try to tag the tail.

Encourage all the players to hold on tight: The line must not break or the dragon will "die." When the head tags the tail, have the head move to the end of the line to become the new tail. Begin a new round with the next player in line as the dragon's head.

Line Tag

Materials: chalk or masking tape for marking the ground

Draw three lines across the width of the playing space. Assign a catcher to stand on each line. Tell the catchers that they will move back and forth along their lines trying to tag the other players. Explain that each catcher must stay on his line. Have the rest of the group begin at one end of the space and try to run to the other end without being tagged. Ask each runner to keep score of how many times she is tagged.

Let the group cross the room twice. Then ask who has managed to cross without being tagged. Choose three new catchers for the next round.

Variations:

- With younger children, place the catchers in the areas between the lines rather than on the lines themselves. Let the children cross the room once. Who got tagged? Then add to the excitement by having more than one catcher in each area.
- The players who are tagged also become catchers and must stay on the line. Have the runners cross the room again and again until the last one is tagged. Who survives the longest?
- To make the game more challenging, have the catchers move along wavy, curving lines instead of straight ones. If these lines cross each other, the catchers can work together and make things very hard for the other players.
- The players who are tagged choose a position between the lines. They stand with legs apart and form barricades for the other players. The barricades cannot move from their spots or tag anyone.

Tease the Wolf

Tell players that this game comes from Peru, a country in South America.

Demonstrate the game by playing the wolf for the first round. Explain that this is a game of tag, and the signal to run is "Yes, I'm ready!"

Have players gather round you in a circle and say, "Wolf, are you ready?" Respond with excuses, such as "I'm brushing my teeth" or "I'm not done with my homework yet." Have players repeat the question until you shout, "Yes, I'm ready!" and begin chasing them. The first player you tag should be the wolf in the next round.

Fishing Nets

Tell the group that in this game, a team of two players will be "It." Invite three volunteers to help you demonstrate. Have two volunteers face each other and hold both hands to form a "fishing net." Then have them raise their joined arms and bring them down to catch the third volunteer between them. Tell the team not to break hands.

Explain that players who are caught should be taken to the "harbor," a place at the side of the playing space. When there are two players in the harbor, they can form a new fishing net and return to the game. The game will continue until the last free player is caught. Choose a pair to be "It" and begin play.

Variations:

- Begin the game with two fishing nets. This makes for more action.
- The two players who are "It" hold hands to form a "fishing rod." With their free hands they can each tag other players. The first "fish" they tag stands between them, and they all join hands to form a chain. When a second player is tagged, she and the player in the middle break away and hold hands to form a new fishing rod. This variation does not use a "harbor."

The Hungry Shark

Tell the group that this game involves three types of player: fish, fishers with nets, and a hungry shark ("It"). Any fish the shark tags becomes the new shark and has to announce the fact by calling out "I am the hungry shark!"

Explain that the fish may find safety in the fishers' nets. Have three volunteers help you demonstrate how the nets work. (See game number 9: "Fishing Nets.")

Choose pairs of players to form the fishing nets. There can be two or more nets, depending on the number of players. In a group of 24 players, four nets will be enough. Explain that each net will be a safe base for two specific fish. Before play begins, have the fishers decide between themselves which two fish will be safe in their net. Their names should remain secret. Point out that fish can try to hide in any net, but each net may not open for them. Players can stay in a net for a count of ten, after which they have to go back into the sea. They can, however, return to the net again.

Choose a shark and begin the game. After there have been five different sharks, have the fishers decide on a new catch and begin the next round. After two rounds choose new players to be fishers.

Note: To ensure that everyone has a safe place in the net during the game, you might add a rule that in each new round the fishers must choose players who have not yet had a turn. Alternatively, you might choose the fish yourself and whisper their names in the fishers' ears.

Back-Hand Tag

Tell players that this game is especially exciting because every player is "It" and can also be tagged. Explain that players must count how many times they tag other people and try to be tagged as little as possible themselves. Demonstrate to players the tricky part: Players must put one hand behind their back, between the shoulder blades, palm facing outwards. Explain that this is the only spot on which players can be tagged.

Use a large play area and make sure there are no obstacles. When the time is up, find out who tagged the most people. This game is all about action: The total number of people anyone tags is less important. As leader, you do not have much chance to see what is going on, so players are on their honor to be honest about their tag-counts. Save this game for groups who know each other well.

Boundary Tag

Materials: chalk or masking tape for marking the ground

Play this tag game in a relatively small space. A twenty-foot square is large enough for 18 players. Draw lines on the ground to indicate the boundaries. Tell players that no one is allowed to go out-of-bounds. Choose a player to be "It" and explain that anyone she tags becomes the new "It." The "Its" will follow each other in quick succession. The limited space makes this game very high-energy, so it is perfect for warming up or letting off steam.

Variations:
- Start the game with two "Its."
- Anyone who goes out of bounds must sit on the sidelines. When three players are out, the first can return to the game.
- A player who has just been tagged must stand on the spot and count to ten out loud before becoming the new "It." Then she can begin chasing people.

Duck-Duck-Goose

Have players sit in a circle on the ground. Demonstrate the game by playing the role of "It" yourself for one or two rounds. Walk slowly around the circle, lightly touching each player you pass on the back and calling out, "duck—duck—duck." Suddenly, call one player "goose" and begin running. Challenge the "goose" to jump up and chase you. If you can run all the way around the circle and sit down in the free space before the goose tags you, the goose starts the next round as "It." If you are tagged, you have to try again and the goose returns to his seat. Once players understand the game, have them play on without you.

Variation: Make sure there is an odd number of players. Choose one player to be "It." Have the other players sit in a spread-out circle and then turn sideways so that pairs of players are sitting back-to-back, touching feet with the players on either side. (See illustration.) Have players put their hands on their legs to keep from tripping the runners. "It" walks around the circle and touches one couple lightly on the heads and begins to run round the circle.

The two players jump up and run in opposite directions around the circle. Who will be first to sit down? The last player to sit begins the next round as "It."

Concentration Games

Concentration games require players to focus on their own movements, on the movements of another player, or on traveling through the space. These games demand a high degree of attention, awareness, and discipline.

It is best to play a concentration game just after a more active game. Make sure the room is quiet, but use music if you feel it will make the players more comfortable. Some people become nervous if they have to work in silence. Do not let these games go on for too long.

Some of the games are played with eyes closed. This directs the attention inward and helps players experience the movements more intensely.

Where Are You?

Materials: two blindfolds; (optional: chalk or masking tape for marking the ground)

Tell the group that children play this game in Botswana, a country in Africa. Draw a large circle on the ground and have players stand along the edges. Alternatively, you might have players arrange chairs into a large circle and sit down. Choose two players to come inside the circle. Explain that one player will be "It" and the other will try to escape, but there is one catch. Each of these players will wear a blindfold and must listen carefully to hear where the other player is. Blindfold the two players, ask the players forming the circle to keep very quiet, and begin play.

If the blindfolded players are about to step outside the circle, the other players can help them by gently turning them around and showing them the right direction. When the player who is "It" finds the other blindfolded player, stop the game and have them take off their blindfolds. Choose two new players to be in the center for the next round.

This game is exciting not just for the blindfolded players, but also for the players around the circle. They may watch with a thrill as the blindfolded players unknowingly brush past each other. Make sure that the players in the circle don't reveal the blindfolded players' locations.

Variations:

- If "It" has difficulty in finding the other player, make the circle a little smaller.
- "It" can call out "Where are you?" and the other player must answer "Here!"

Freeze!

♪ **Music:** fast and rhythmic music

Play music and encourage players to move around the room in any way they like, as long as they don't touch each other. Tell players that whenever the music stops, they should freeze exactly as they are. They must stay in the same position until the music starts again. Explain that anyone who moves is out and stands at the side. When a fourth player is out, invite the first one to join the game again, so there will never be more than three players standing at the side. (Adjust this number to fit the size of the group.)

Variations:

- When the music stops, players move as slowly as possible.
- Challenge players to move in ways that will make holding their positions difficult—skipping or hopping on one foot, for example. How long can they freeze? Don't let the frozen players remain in position for longer than a count of eight.

Mirror Game

♪ **Music:** peaceful and/or relaxing New Age music

Have players form pairs and stand face-to-face. Invite one partner in each pair to pretend to be a mirror and imitate everything the other partner does. Encourage the other partner to begin making slow and familiar movements—for instance, she might pretend to wash her face, brush her teeth, get dressed, and so on. The partner should then feel free to improvise motions for the "mirror" to imitate: Her movements do not have to represent a concrete situation. After a while, tell the players to switch roles.

You might invite players to improvise a dance based on this principle. In this case, ask the partners to move a little farther apart so that they have room to move.

Variations:

* With mature players, invite both partners to act as mirrors and imitate each other. Have partners face each other and concentrate. Some kind of movement will begin of its own accord. The players mirror each other without either of them obviously taking the initiative. In fact, each one will be leader and follower in turn, but the roles will change so quickly that it will seem as if they are moving simultaneously.

* You can change this game slightly to make it into a guessing-game. Ask each pair to agree on a secret signal for changing roles. Suggest that they choose a simple movement for their signal, such as raising one hand. Let the players practice using their signals.

  Next assign the pairs to two teams. One team continues to play the mirror game, using their secret signals to change roles as they go along. The other team watches to try to discover the secret signals. After 3 minutes, have the observers guess what the signals are. Then have the teams switch places.

One Step Forward, One Step Back

Materials: two different musical instruments; chalk or tape for marking the ground

Use chalk or tape to mark a line down the center of the room. Have players stand side by side along the line. Display two musical instruments and tell players that the sounds of the instruments will tell them how to move. Play one of the instruments and explain that this sound means take one step forward. Play the other instrument and explain that this sound means take one step back. Have players practice this once or twice.

Tell players that the object of the game is to follow the signals and keep their steps equal in size: If they do, they will end up back on the center line. Then begin the game. Be sure to make the two signals an equal number of times; for instance, drum-drum-bell-drum-bell-bell. Then check whether everyone made it back to the center line.

Variations:

- Once players have mastered the game with eyes open, have them play with eyes closed. Remind them to try to keep their steps equal in size. When you come to the end of a round, have players open their eyes to see who reached the center line.
- You can make the game more difficult by having players listen to a series of signals before each move. For example, you might play the sequence drum-drum-bell-drum, and then have players move.

Slow Motion

♪ **Music:** slow, meditative piano music

Have players lie on the floor, close their eyes, and relax. Then ask players to keep their eyes closed and stand up as slowly as they possibly can. Tell them to open their eyes when they are finished and watch the others who are still getting up.

Point out that there is still movement, even in slow motion. Players must move in order to stand up. Repeat the game a few times.

Variations:

- Use restful music as a background; this will help players move slowly and smoothly.
- Combine this game with fantasy images. You might have players pretend to be seeds slowly growing into trees, buds opening into flowers, or statues coming to life.
- Have players move in other ways: They might roll over, raise their legs into the air, or lie down from a standing position.

Note: Play this game when everyone is nicely warmed up. This makes it easier for players to control their movements.

Forest Tag

Materials: a blindfold; chalk for marking the ground

Tell players that in this game of tag, they will pretend to be trees in a forest. Have players spread out and choose spaces. Pass out chalk and ask each player to draw a circle on the ground around her right foot. Explain that this foot is now rooted to the ground, and it must stay inside the circle. Invite players to experiment to see what motions they can make without moving the right foot.

Choose one player to be "It," let her leave her circle, and blindfold her. Give "It" 2 minutes to tag as many "trees" as she can. The other players, who can see "It" coming, can make evasive movements as long as they do not move the right foot. Each player tagged and each right foot that moves from its spot earns "It" one point. Make sure that "It" does not hurt herself.

Variation: Draw lines on the floor to create a smaller play area— for instance, 6 x 4 yards for 16 players. Have the players spread out so that they can just touch each other. Otherwise, the game is the same.

20

Night Prowlers

Materials: chalk or masking tape for marking the ground; a blindfold for each player

Tell players that in this game of tag, only two players are runners and everyone else is "It." Mark out a long but narrow play area: for instance, 3 x 8 yards for 18 players. Choose two runners and explain that they must start at one end of the area and reach the other end without being tagged. Ask the other players to spread out and choose spots where they cannot touch each other. Tell these players that they cannot move from their places to chase the runners, but they can wave their arms around slowly. Demonstrate the slow tempo of the arm movements and have players practice for a minute. Then tell players about the catch: Everyone but the runners must wear a blindfold! Pass out the blindfolds and begin the game.

Point out that everyone should be as quiet as possible in order to hear the prowlers (runners) better. Can they slip through without being tagged? Let new pairs try in succession.

Variations:

- The game is easier if the two players crossing the room make soft buzzing sounds.
- You might also have the blindfolded players make a certain kind of sound—mechanical sounds, for instance.

Freezing and Thawing

♪ **Music:** slow classical music

Play slow music and have players stand in a circle, frozen in place.
Choose a part of the body and tell players that this part has thawed
and can move again. Encourage players to move that part in any way
they like.

Gradually allow players to move other parts of the body: You
might begin with fingers and move on to the hands, arms, torso, and
head. Now tell players that their bodies are slowly freezing again.
Name the same body parts in reverse order and have players freeze
each one in turn until their bodies are completely still again.

Repeat this game a few times, freezing different body parts. Let
the players choose a new starting position each time.

Variation: Let different players suggest the type of movement to
be made with each newly thawed part of the body. Have the whole
group follow these movements.

Don't Touch

Materials: chalk or masking tape for marking the ground

♪ **Music:** up-tempo music

Use chalk or tape to mark the boundaries of a small play area—for instance, a 20-foot square for 18 people. Have players spread out and move to the music without touching each other. Call out different ways for the players to move. You might have players move in the following ways:

- walk on tiptoes
- walk with outstretched arms
- walk backwards
- crawl on hands and knees
- walk on their heels

Remind players of the main rule in this game: They cannot touch anyone. Each player has to concentrate his attention on his own movements.

Variations: You can make the game more difficult by

- choosing music with a faster tempo
- repeatedly making the play area smaller.

Moving Joints

Ask players to try walking without bending their knees. Point out that without joints, our bodies would be completely stiff and unable to move. Tell players that in this game, they will explore all the movements made possible by their different joints.

Have players sit in a circle. You will move the joints in groups, working through them one by one from bottom to top. Invite players to move their toe joints. Encourage them to try out all the things their toes can do. Players might pinch their toes together, spread them apart, or move only one toe at a time. Watch the movements different players are making and point out new ones so that everyone can try them out. Put the emphasis on the feeling and the discovery of the movement. The idea is for the players themselves to discover the various movements possible.

Continue through the ankle and knee joints to the hips. Finally have players shake out their legs. Now have everyone stand up. Invite players to see what movements they can make with their hip joints: for instance, turning circles or tipping the pelvis backwards and forwards.

Move on to the knuckles, wrists, elbows, and shoulders. Keep pointing out new movements that different players have discovered. Challenge players to do the movements at different speeds.

End with the joints of the neck and backbone. Make sure players explore these movements gently and cautiously, as it is easy to strain neck and back muscles.

Variations:

- Use the game with young children as part of a fantasy story. Tell the children they are puppets, and the puppeteer is on vacation. Now they can find out for themselves what movements they are able to make. Make a guessing game out of it: You might ask, "Who knows a joint that you can move in your arm?"

- With mature players, this activity can also be used for an improvised dance. Play peaceful music. Have players spread out and work independently. Name various joints. As players dance, they accent each joint you name.

Hiding and Guessing Games

Children love to hide things, to search for things, and to solve mysteries. The games in this category meet these needs very well. The games are also good for older players. The emphasis is not so much on success as on learning to observe carefully.

To solve the puzzles involved in these games, players must view things from different angles, trust their own intuition, and be willing to seek a solution in an unexpected direction. These are important conditions for the development of creativity.

What Am I Writing?

Tell players that they can write in the air. Invite them to pretend they have big sticks of chalk in their writing hands. Have them write their names in the air in big letters. Depending on the age of the group, you might have them try writing in printing or cursive, and in capitals or lower case letters. Let players practice writing in the air for a minute. There is always the risk that some players might make mischief by spelling out inappropriate words. You may want to make

a rule that players can write only words they would be allowed to say in the classroom: Any player breaking this rule is out of the game for good.

Have players form pairs and stand one behind the other. Ask the player in front to write a word in the air. The player behind has to guess what it is. Then have partners change places.

(See game number 25: "What Are You Writing?" and game number 26: "The Secret Word" for more opportunities to write in the air.)

Variations:

- Have younger children write just one capital letter in the air.
- Have players write numbers or simple math problems instead of words.
- You might have older players stand face-to-face and try to decipher the "mirror-writing."

What Are You Writing?

See game number 24: "What Am I Writing?" for an introduction to writing in the air. Ask players to form pairs. Have one partner stand behind the other and hold the other partner's "writing arm" as if it were a big pencil. Explain that the player in back should use the arm of the player in front to write a word in the air. The player in front has to guess what the word is.

Variation: Invite partners to try to write a sentence together without discussing it in advance. Explain that partners should take turns writing words in the air using each other's arms. Ask the partners not to talk. Encourage them to choose words that will link together to form a sentence. If the player in front cannot guess a word the first time, it can be repeated. Challenge pairs to write the group's longest sentence.

The Secret Word

♪ **Music:** waltz music if desired (do not use music with lyrics)

See game number 24: "What Am I Writing?" for an introduction to writing in the air. Create groups of five players. Ask each group to work together to choose a five-letter word and assign one letter to each group member. Groups should keep their words secret. Have each group spell out the secret word by walking across the room one by one, writing their letters in the air over and over. Ask the other players to try to guess the word.

You may wish to inspire the movement with music.

Variation: Have the whole group cross the room at the same time. They will have more freedom of movement and the observers will have a challenging puzzle to solve.

Make the Right Move

Materials: cards with movement instructions; masking tape

Write simple movement instructions on cards. You might include the following instructions: *clap your hands, jump, make a bow, turn your head, stand on one leg, kneel, hop, wave your arms, crawl, walk backwards, lie down, put your hand on your head,* and so on. You can use the cards to play many different games (see game number 28: "The Secret Movement"). Use cardboard or stiff paper so that the cards will last. Write the instructions clearly in large letters: They should be legible from 6 feet away.

First read the cards aloud. Encourage players to remember the instructions. Pass the cards out and ask players to keep the instructions on their cards secret. Then have each player tape his card face-out on another player's back without telling the player what it says.

Tell players that they must guess which movement instructions are taped to their backs. Explain that they should show other players their cards and then try out different movements. The other players should watch the movements and tell whether each guess is right, wrong, or very close but not quite right. Players who have guessed correctly can sit down.

You can join the game by helping players who have not yet found the right answer. You might keep a separate list of all the instructions on the cards, so that you can read it aloud later in the game if players need more help.

The Secret Movement

Materials: movement cards

♪ **Music:** up-tempo pop music for dancing

Pass out movement cards (see game number 27: "Make the Right Move"). Ask players to peek at their cards without letting anyone else see what is written on them. Play music and invite the players to dance however they like. Tell them there is only one rule: While dancing, each player must make the movement that was written on his card. Tell the players to bring the movement into their dance several times by doing it in different ways: They might do it quickly, then extremely slowly, then subtly, and finally with a great flourish.

Divide the group roughly in two. Have half the players sit down and watch the other half dance. Ask the dancing group to demonstrate their secret movements a number of times in different ways. The watchers should try to guess each dancer's movement. With a large group, you may want to assign one dancer to each observer. Stop the music, have the observers make their guesses, and then let the groups switch places.

Who Is the Leader?

Have players stand in a circle. Join the circle and ask players to imitate you as you make a simple movement over and over. Then change the movement and encourage players to follow along. Repeat a few times to let players practice copying. Then have one player leave the room. Choose a new leader to initiate the movements. Encourage the leader to use movements that are easy to repeat—for instance, nod your head, wobble your leg, raise and lower your arm. The leader should keep changing the movement, and everyone should try to follow as quickly as possible.

Bring the player who was outside the room back to stand in the center of the circle. Give the player three chances to guess who the secret leader is.

Notes:

- The group should make it difficult to guess who is leading the movements. Discourage players from looking directly at the leader. Have them try to follow each change in movement immediately. For the youngest groups this is very difficult: The players almost all look directly at the secret leader. The still have great fun playing the game.
- With groups of older players, suggest using small movements. These are harder to imitate.

Emotion
Duet

Materials: cards with emotions written on them (see below)

♪ **Music:** various musical excerpts (classical, pop, and New Age)

Choose several emotions and write each one on two cards. You might use the following emotions: *happy, angry, tired, vain, shy, frightened, excited, miserable*. Mark one card of each pair with a dot. Make sure that there is a card for each player.

Pass out the cards. Ask players to peek at their cards without letting anyone else see what is written on them. Explain that there are two players for each emotion. Have each player notice whether his card has a dot on it. Tell the players with the dotted cards that it is their job to find the other player who has the same emotion. Begin the music and ask every player to move in a way that shows the emotion on his card. Encourage players to watch each other closely. After a while, have the players with dotted cards stand behind someone who they think has the same emotion.

Let the groups continue to move. They may have formed threes or fours. Give these players the chance to switch. Then stop the music and see if the emotion of the player behind is the same as that of the one in front. This can be done by asking each couple to give a short demonstration. Gather the cards, shuffle them, and let the players pick new cards for the next round.

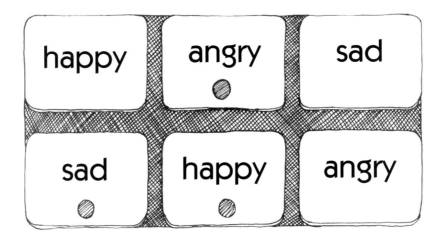

Variations:

- To adapt this game for large groups, make trios or quartets with the same emotion. Be sure that for each emotion, every card but one has a dot on it.
- Ask players to ignore the dots on their cards and simply move with their emotion. Have two players stand at the side and observe the other players. Encourage the moving players to exaggerate their emotions. After 2 minutes, the observers have 30 seconds to make groups from the players they think have the same emotion. Have them name the players who belong together.

The Moving Alphabet

Invite the group to imagine that the letters of the alphabet could move. Point out that just as each letter has its own sound, each letter would have its own way of moving.

Tell the group that they are going to move like letters. You might suggest a few starting points for translating a letter into movement:

- the shape of the letter—a U might make U-turns, while an A might walk with legs stiffly splayed out
- the sound of the letter—an S might move like a hissing snake ("ssss")
- a word beginning with the same letter—a B might *bounce*

For those learning to read, this game can be an enjoyable way of practicing the letters of the alphabet. First have the group act out the letters one by one. Then tell a story in which several letters have an adventure and let everyone act it out at the same time.

Variations:

- Invite the group to put on a letter parade. Assign letters to groups of two or three players. Give them a little time to rehearse their movements and then it's showtime!
- Play a guessing game. Have groups choose a word and present it letter by letter. The observers have to guess what word walked in front of them.

Three Actions, One Job

Materials: (optional: cards and pens for variation)

Have players form groups of three. Ask each group of three to choose an active job, such as cook or window cleaner. Then have each player choose a movement or action that is characteristic of that job. For instance, the group might choose the job of window-cleaner, and the players might choose setting up a ladder, wiping a window, and using a squeegee as their actions.

Have the groups demonstrate their actions to the others one by one. Ask the spectators to guess what each job is.

Variations:

- Suggest that players exaggerate the movements.
- Play one round of the game as above. Then pass out pens, give each player a card, and have players write down the job and action they chose (for example, "Cook: stirring the pan"). Collect all the cards, shuffle them, and pass them out again. Players should not show their cards to anyone else. Have players spread out around the room and perform the movements on their cards. Encourage players to watch each other closely and join up with the others belonging to the same job. This variation can be used for forming groups to play a new game.

Alphabet Soup

Depending on the size of the group, have players form groups of two or three. Divide up the letters of the alphabet so that each group has several consecutive letters. Explain that groups will use their bodies to make each letter. Ask players to make sure that every group member is part of each letter and to form the letters lying down. Let the groups work simultaneously.

Variations:

- Have groups make the sound of each letter as they form it with their bodies.
- Tell the group that in this game, they will use their bodies to create puzzles. Assign a five-letter word to each group. Let group members work out how to form the letters. Then have each group present its word to the others. The spectators try to guess the word. Point out instances in which different groups form the same letter in completely different ways.

Bump Jump

Divide the group into two teams of roughly equal size. Invite one team to talk amongst themselves and come up with a verb that can be acted out. Suggest that they choose a verb that names a physical activity, such as *jump, run,* or *spin*. (In order to prevent teams from choosing an inappropriate word, you may want to have the team whisper their verb to you before play begins.) Next, help the team think of a word that rhymes with the verb they chose, such as *bump, fun,* or *win*.

The first team then tells the other team the rhyming word. The other team has three chances to guess the original verb and act it out. If they guess correctly, they win a point. Have the teams switch roles for the next round.

A Present for the Czar

Materials: chalk or tape for marking the ground

Tell players that this game comes from Russia, a country in Eastern Europe, and *czar* is the Russian word for "king." Use chalk or tape to mark two parallel lines, one at each end of the play space. Choose a player to begin the game as the czar, and explain that everyone else is a peasant. Have the czar move out of earshot while the peasants work together to come up with an imaginary present for the czar. Then have the czar stand behind the line at one end of the space. Ask the peasants to gather round him, but not too closely.

Tell players that when the game begins, the peasants should use movements to show what their present is: they might hold it to show how heavy, soft, or delicate it is, or they might use it to show its purpose. Explain that the czar must try to guess what the present is. When he guesses correctly, he can cross the line and chase the peasants. If the czar tags a peasant before she can reach the line at the far end of the space, that peasant becomes the czar for the next round.

Reaction Games

These games depend on quick reactions. They require the participants to be fully present in the moment. Players must not only pay attention, but also keep every muscle on the alert. Only then is a quick reaction possible. Players cannot let their minds wander to such subjects as tonight's dinner or what the other children think about them.

In addition, these games encourage spontaneity by inviting players to react when they least expect it.

The Turning Circle

Have all of the players except one sit on chairs in a circle. Ask the player without a chair to stand in the center. Explain that this player will give orders to the group. If he says "turn left," then everyone has to move one chair to the left. If he says "turn right," the whole group must move one chair to the right. Let players practice this once or twice.

Tell the player in the center to watch for players who react too slowly. If any chair remains open long enough, the player in the center should rush to sit down on it. Point out that the player in the center can try to catch the players unawares by calling out orders suddenly or in quick succession. Explain that any player who loses his seat will move to the center and give the orders for the next round.

Switch Tag
with Cat and Mouse

Tell the group that this is a tag game in which the role of "It" changes constantly. Choose one player to be the cat ("It") and one player to be the mouse. Have the other players stand in a wide circle with their legs apart.

Tell players that the cat will run around the outside of the circle trying to catch the mouse. The mouse can run away, or she can escape by crawling into a "mouse hole" (i.e., between someone's legs). Tell players that when this happens, everyone switches roles. The player whose legs were the "hole" now becomes the cat. The player who was the mouse takes his place in the circle. The player who was originally the cat is now the mouse and must run away quickly so as not to be caught. Encourage the players to switch roles often; it makes the game very exciting.

38

Follow the Leader

Materials: (optional: props such as crepe-paper ribbons, sheets of newspaper, and paper towel rolls)

♪ **Music:** marching band music

This game has been a playground favorite for many years. Choose one player to be the leader, and have the others follow him in a long line. All the players imitate the leader's changing movements. The following variations help make the game more interesting and challenging for older players.

Variations:

- Have several lines following different leaders, so that the lines can weave through each other.
- Agree on a signal that means the leader should go to the back of the line. The next player in line then becomes the leader. Use the signal periodically to give every player a turn.

- Move from individual movements to form larger and larger groups. First, have everyone move around the room individually in whatever way they like. Then ask the players to form pairs with a leader and a follower. Next, have pairs group together into lines of four. Continue until the whole group forms one long line.
- Vary the style of music.
- Provide each player with the same prop, such as crepe-paper ribbons, sheets of newspaper, or paper towel rolls. Ask them to make their movements using these materials.

39

Newspaper Dance

Materials: newspapers or pieces of cardboard

♪ **Music:** lively music, such as disco or salsa

Give each child a piece of cardboard or several sheets of newspaper. Have children fold the newspapers twice, spread out around the room, and sit on the papers. Play music and invite children to hop around the room. Have them try not to touch the newspapers. Tell children that when the music stops, they must sit down on a newspaper as quickly as possible. Tell them that they don't need to sit in the places where they started.

When everyone is sitting, begin the music again for the next round.

Variations:

- Tell the children to move in different ways: They might jump like frogs, slink like cats, or slither like snakes.
- With older children this can be played as an elimination game. Use the same principle, but remove one newspaper after each round. Whoever is left without a seat is out of the game.

Four Walls

Materials: four sheets of construction paper in different colors; tape

Have children sit in a circle in the middle of the room. Tape one sheet of colored construction paper to each of the room's four walls. Explain that you will tell a story that includes different colors. Each time you mention a color, players should run to touch the wall with that color. Then have them come back to the circle and continue telling your story. You might add to the fun by occasionally mentioning colors that are not shown on the walls.

Variations:

- Instead of colors, you might use cards marked with numbers or adjectives, such as *cold, warm, lukewarm, hot,* or *large, huge, small, tiny*.

- Tell a story that features at least four animals. Explain that each animal moves in a different way. Before you begin, show children how each animal moves: Walk in that manner to a wall and hang up a picture of the animal. Walk back in the same way. When an animal is mentioned in the story, the children walk to the appropriate wall imitating the movements you made.

Streets and Avenues

Materials: whistle or other sound signal

This game requires at least 14 players. Choose one player to be the cat and another to be the mouse. Divide the rest of the group into three or more equal rows, each an arm's length behind the next. Have the players in each row hold hands and space themselves an

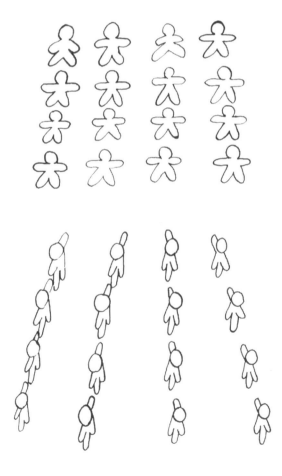

arm's length apart. Line up the players so that they are exactly in line with the players in front and behind (see illustration). Then ask everyone to drop hands and turn to face right. Have them hold hands with the players now standing next to them. This way the avenues become streets and vice-versa. Agree on a whistle or other sound that will signal players to turn and change hands. Practice this a few times. Begin slowly and gradually speed up.

Now introduce the cat and the mouse. Explain that the cat has to try to catch the mouse. The cat and the mouse can only run along the avenues and streets; they cannot use the rest of the room or break through the walls of players. The cat can only catch the mouse if they are in the same street or avenue; she cannot reach over the arms into another street. When the cat catches the mouse, they exchange roles. After a time, stop the game and choose new players to be the cat and the mouse.

Variations:

- Have the cat attempt to catch two mice.
- Have one of the players sit out and give the signal for the streets to change into avenues. You could have the player stand either with his back to the game, or facing it. In the latter case, the player can influence the strategies of the cat and the mouse.
- Agree on a different sound (for example, the ring of a bell) that signals the cat and mouse to switch roles during the game. This adds an extra dimension to the game.

Introduction Games

When a group of strangers acts uncomfortable and shy with each other, these games can help break the ice. Some of the games also help players learn everyone's name. Introductory games help groups move past the inevitable beginning stage of politeness and formality. The games are short and simple. They create a pleasant and informal atmosphere. They encourage spontaneity and playfulness in the participants. Everyone takes part, so group members get to know each other quickly.

These are real group games: The group is constantly working together, and this strengthens the feeling of unity.

The Empty Chair

Have players sit on chairs in a circle. Ask them to call out their own names one by one. Then place an extra chair in the circle. Ask the player to the right of the empty chair to slap it and call out the name of someone in the circle. Have the player whose name was called run to sit on the empty chair.

Now a different chair is empty. Have the person to the right of this chair pat it and call out another name, and so on. Practice this with the group. The idea is that players react quickly and become familiar with the new names. If necessary, have the group members call out their names again.

Remove the empty chair from the circle and select one player to stand in the center and be "It." Now this player's chair is empty. Play the game according to the description above, but this time "It" tries to reach the empty chair before the player to the right pats the chair and calls out a name. If "It" does not reach the chair in time, he tries to steal the next empty seat, and so on. If a player sitting to the right of an empty seat reacts too slowly and doesn't call out a name before "It" sits down, that player has to take his place in the middle.

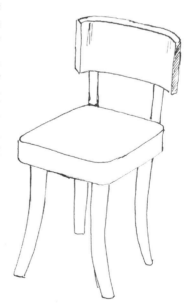

Too Late, Neighbor

Have players sit in a circle. Assign each player a number in sequence, beginning with one. Ask number one to begin by calling out another player's number. Have the person whose number was called call another number as quickly as possible, and so on. Tell players that they cannot call out numbers immediately above or below their own. Practice this until everyone reacts quickly.

Then introduce a new rule. The person whose number is one higher than the number called can try to beat his neighbor by naming a new number before she does. (For example, if a player calls out "seven," number eight can try to call out a new number before number seven gets the chance.)

If the player whose number was called reacts too slowly and does not call out a number before her neighbor, she goes to sit on the chair of the person with the highest number. Everyone in between moves over one place: These players now all have new numbers. Have number one begin the next round by calling out a number. It is great fun when number two is too quick for number one. In that case all the players switch chairs and everyone gets a new number!

Note: If the players have difficulty in remembering the changing numbers, you can put numbers on the chairs.

Group Seven

♪ **Music:** cheerful music, such as Dixieland jazz

This game allows players to be active and get to know each other in small groups at the same time. Ask players to move around the room in any way they like. Encourage them to use the whole space. Tell players, "Don't walk around in a group or form clumps, but try to make sure there is no empty space on the floor. If you see a space, go and fill it." Play some cheerful music; this creates a good feeling and invites the players to skip or dance.

Tell the players that you will stop the music every so often and ask them to form groups of different sizes. Explain that if you call out "Group 2," they should quickly form groups of two players; "Group 3" means groups of three players, and so on. Anyone left over should go to stand with you. Explain that there is one exception. If you call out "Group 7," instead of forming groups, the players must sit on the floor as quickly as possible.

When the players have formed groups, assign a short introduction exercise for each group to perform.

For instance, you might ask players to:
- shake hands with each other
- name the street on which they live
- name their favorite hobbies
- name the people they most admire
- find three similarities shared by every member of the group
- pose together as they would for a group photo

Have the leftover players who did not fit into a group help you watch to see whether the assignments are done well. Then start the music again and have players spread out. Play this game a few times, calling out different-sized groups each time. Finish the game with groups of the size you want for the next game.

The Buzzing Circle

Have players stand in a large circle, close their eyes, and make a soft buzzing sound. Ask them to hold their arms out in front of them and slowly walk towards the center. Have them reach out until they find two hands to hold. When a player has found two hands, she should keep holding them, open her eyes, and stop buzzing. The players who have not yet found two hands continue to buzz and the other players help them to find hands without speaking.

Name Game

This simple game has many possible variations. Have players stand in a circle. Ask them to call out their names one by one and make a movement at the same time. The whole group immediately repeats both the name and the movement.

Variations:

- Encourage each player to choose a movement that tells something about him: for instance, an action based on his favorite sport or hobby.

- Have players sing their names. You might demonstrate by singing your own name in a few different styles: perhaps Broadway, rap, opera, country, or gospel.

- Have players say their names softly and make small movements. The group should repeat these loudly with large gestures.

- Have the group repeat each name and movement three times: first very softly, then a little more loudly, and finally very loudly.

- Invite advanced players to use alliteration. Tell each player to say his name together with a feature or characteristic that begins with the same letter: for instance, Soccer Sarah, Powerful Pablo, Laughing Liam, Math-whiz Masako, and so on.

  In this variation some players may take a long time to find a word. With the added pressure of everyone looking at them, it becomes even harder. It is a good idea to give everyone time to think before the beginning of the round and start only when everyone has thought of a word.

I'm Going on a Journey

Sit down and have players join you in a circle on the floor. Say, "I'm going on a journey, but first I have to wash the windows," and make a wiping motion. Invite the player to your right to repeat your words and motion, and then add another thing he has to do, accompanied by an appropriate movement. For example, the player might say, "I'm going on a journey, but first I have to wash the windows and feed the cat," as he makes a wiping motion and then pantomimes opening a can.

Each subsequent player should repeat all the actions mentioned as he makes all the movements, and then add one of his own. The list becomes longer and longer. When everyone has had a turn, have the whole group repeat the entire series together.

Note: You might allow players in a large group to repeat only the last five actions.

Name Tag

Tell players that this game is called "name tag." Explain that this is because runners can escape being tagged by standing with their legs apart and calling out the name of another player. Before you begin, have players stand in a circle and call out their own names one by one. Then choose a player to be "It." If she tags someone, that player becomes the new "It." The new "It" must yell his own name before chasing the other players.

Players who stand with legs apart and call out the name of another player are "safe" and cannot be tagged. They should not call their own name or the name of the player who is "It." Players who are "safe" must remain standing with legs apart until another player releases them to rejoin the game. Players can release "safe" players by crawling between their legs.

In a Knot

Have players stand in a circle holding hands. Make a break in the circle. The player on your right is now at the front of a long, curving chain, and the player on your left is at the back of the chain. Lead the front of the chain in and out through the back of the chain, weaving over and under the players' linked hands. The chain will begin to tangle into a knot.

At a certain moment the knot will become so tangled that it can tighten no further. Then have the players at the front and back of the chain join hands. Invite the group to move slowly and carefully to untangle itself and form a circle again. Encourage players to try to do this without breaking hands. If it really cannot be done, then in the interest of safety, allow players to release each other's hands.

Variation: Ask two players to leave the room. Have the group make a knot as above, with one exception. This time the players at each end of the knot do not join hands; instead they hide their hands in the middle of the knot. When the knot is tied tightly, invite the two players to come back. Have them try to untie the knot without parting any of the hands.

Cooperation Games

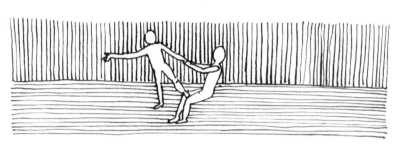

Working together can give people a wonderful boost in confidence. We realize we can achieve more together than we can as individuals. Ideally, people would always cooperate. But working together is not that simple.

In these cooperation games, the focus is on interactions among the players. How do they react to one another? How can they find a solution together? Does the group take advantage of individual players' different strengths in playing the game? Or, are players' differences magnified so that they interfere with cooperation?

Most cooperation games are not geared toward producing an end result, and there may not be a winner. It is a good idea to point this out when introducing and ending the games. The players who work together are the winners!

Don't Drop the Ball

Materials: one ball for every two players

♪ **Music:** peaceful New Age or classical music

Have players form pairs. Provide each pair with a soft, flexible ball. Challenge partners to work together to hold the ball without using their hands. Let partners experiment with holding the ball in different ways, such as pressed between their foreheads, arms, backs, or knees.

Then encourage the players to discover how they can move while still holding the ball between them. Can they squat, sit, walk, or jump? Give various suggestions and let the pairs show each other what they have discovered and try out what they have seen others do.

Variations:

- Try the same activity with two balls held between each pair.
- Instead of a ball, try other materials: boxes, toilet paper rolls, balloons, building blocks, and so on. Let players explore the differences.
- Invite partners to dance with the ball. Play restful music. Encourage partners to do their best not to drop the ball.
- Have partners do a dance in which the ball moves. For instance, partners might begin with the ball between their foreheads and finish with it between their backs. Let half the group watch, and then have them trade places. It is interesting to see how the partners manage to do this. Concentration on the ball can combine with music to produce very beautiful movements.

Players older than 12 might try to recreate the dance without the ball. Encourage partners to make the same movements and keep the same distance apart as they would if the ball were between them.

Push Me — Pull You

Divide the group into pairs of roughly equal physical size. Have partners squat on the ground facing each other and grasp one another by the arms. Tell the group that each player should push and pull his partner as if he were trying to make her lose her balance. Explain that there is one catch: Each player has the responsibility of making sure that his partner never actually tumbles over.

Explain that the point of this game is daring to take risks together. Players explore how far they can push each other without actually causing a fall. It may look as if the players are trying their hardest to push each other over. Point out that in reality they are taking good care of each other. Have the group repeat this game a few times, changing partners for each round.

Note: This game can make for an interesting discussion. You might ask: "Was it hard to find a balance between being daring and taking care of your partner? Did you leave it to the other player to take the initiative, or did you take it yourself? How was the game different with different partners?"

Headgear

Materials: one book for each player

Pass out books and have players balance them on their heads. Invite players to move around the room while doing their best to keep the books from falling. Explain that if a player's book falls, she must freeze on the spot and wait for another player to replace it. Tell players there is one catch: When helping other players, they must make sure their own books do not fall, or they will also be frozen. (You might allow younger children to steady their own books when helping other players.)

Once players have mastered walking around, give them various assignments: turn around, sit down, walk fast, walk backwards, walk on tiptoes, and so on.

Variation: Play a tag game in which everyone balances a book on her head, including "It." Tagged players must put their books on the floor and freeze. Tagged players and players who have dropped their books can be freed only if another player replaces the book. There is one exception: "It" can replace her own book if it falls, but she can only do this five times. On the sixth fall, count how many players are frozen and begin the next round.

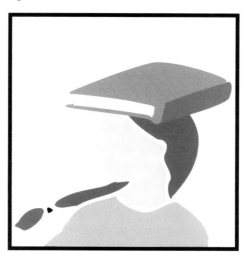

Balloon Toss

Materials: balloons; a stopwatch

Have players form groups of three. Give each group a balloon and challenge them to keep it floating in the air for as long as possible. Explain that players must tap the balloon, not grab it, and no player can touch the balloon twice in a row. Once a group's balloon has touched the ground three times, that group should sit down and watch the others. Which group can last the longest?

Variations:

- Challenge players to keep the balloon in the air using only their knees, feet, heads, or another part of the body.
- Give each group two balloons to keep in the air. Time them with a stopwatch.
- Have the entire group keep as many balloons as possible in the air. Record the time that elapses before the last balloon touches the ground. Let the group try a few times to break its own record.

Marionette Game

If a marionette is available, display one to players before you begin. Tell the group to imagine that you are a marionette, with imaginary strings about 6 inches long attached to your head, elbows, hands, knees, and feet. Choose a volunteer puppeteer to help you demonstrate. Explain that the volunteer can make you move your body by "pulling" on the strings. Let her try causing a few simple movements: She might make you raise your arm or take a step. When the puppeteer lets go of a string, maintain your position: Point out that you do not collapse as a real marionette would. Tell players that marionette and puppeteer must cooperate to make this game work.

Have players form pairs: one marionette and one puppeteer. Let the pairs practice until they have the hang of it. Then have the marionettes lie down and challenge the puppeteers to make them stand up. Encourage players to remain silent. Then have the marionettes and puppeteers switch places and play the game again.

Variations:

- Invite pairs to perform their "puppet shows" as other members of the group watch.
- Help players concentrate by playing soft music.
- Give the pairs new assignments: Have the puppeteers move the marionettes from standing to lying down, or from lying down to sitting on a chair. You may want to assign a series of movements, such as stand, then walk, then sit.
- Challenge the pairs to include emotions: The puppeteers might move the marionettes from sitting miserably to standing happily. Pairs may want to practice the different positions separately and then add the nuances.

55

Fancy Footwork

♪ **Music:** peaceful New Age music

Have players remove their shoes and lie on their backs in pairs, with the soles of their feet touching. Encourage partners to try to feel each other's feet. Then give assignments for the pairs to carry out. Soft music will increase the concentration in this game. You might say the following:

- Push gently against your partner's feet. Can you feel the soles, the heels, and the toes? Can you feel the big toes?
- Try to "bicycle" (move as if pedaling a bicycle) without losing contact with your partner's feet.
- Try to roll all the way over without letting your feet come apart.

Variations:

- Ask one partner in each pair to make slow movements with his feet while the other follows. Encourage players to keep silent. Have partners change roles after a little while.
- Older players can carry out the above assignment without first deciding who will lead and who will follow. Each of the partners will automatically take the initiative at different times. If this works well, neither partner will be able to say which one of them took the initiative; the movements seem to happen of their own accord.

Balloon Round-Up

Materials: one balloon per player; a rope at least 20-feet long; (optional: two colors of balloon and two colors of ribbon— enough for half the players to wear one color and half to wear the other)

Loop the rope to form a large circle in the center of the room. Pass out the balloons. Have each player blow up a balloon and place it on the floor outside the circle. Encourage players to spread the balloons over the whole room. Then have players sit on the ground around the edge of the circle. Tell players that the object of the game is to get all of the balloons into the circle. Explain that there is one catch: Players must use only their feet and legs to move the balloons. They can kick the balloons or catch them between their legs.

The game sounds simple, but very often when a new balloon comes into the circle, it makes some of the others roll out again.

Variations:
- Forbid players from entering the circle.
- Divide the group into two teams. Have the players on each team tie colored ribbons on their ankles, so they can recognize each other. Use two colors of balloons, one for each team. Explain that the winning team will be the one that gets all of its own balloons into the circle first. One tactic players might use is to try to kick the other team's balloons out of the circle.

The Narrow Bridge

Materials: benches; tumbling mats

Have players form two teams of equal size and line up at opposite ends of a bench. Place tumbling mats on either side of the bench. Tell players that each team must walk across the bench to the other side without falling. Explain that there is a catch: Two players—one from each team—will cross at the same time, moving in opposite directions. Point out that the players will meet in the middle and

must help each other pass without falling. Tell players that if they do slip off the bench, they should simply climb back on in the same place.

Although there are two teams, this game is about cooperation rather than competition. The other players watch how their team-mates do. If you are working with a large group, you may want to divide the group into four teams and either use two benches or have the teams take turns.

Variations:
- Have players sing a song as they cross the bridge. Players should try to keep singing as they pass in the middle. It helps if both teams sing the same song.
- Challenge players to carry something to the other side, such as balls, balloons, or sticks.

Hats Off to Teamwork!

Materials: one hat for every player

Tell players that this game is similar to one played in Israel, a country in the Middle East. Form two or more teams of equal size and hand out one hat to every player. Each team should place its hats in a pile and stand in a circle around the pile. Tell players that the first team with a hat on every player's head wins. Then tell them about the catch: Players must clasp their hands behind their backs; they cannot use their hands to put on the hats. Point out that teams will need to work together to put hats onto one another. Suggest that, for example, one player might steady a hat with her feet while another stoops to place his head inside. When every team member is wearing a hat on her head, the team should release their hands and clap loudly to signal that they have won.

Note: Stiff hats made from felt, straw, or paper work best for this game; knitted hats are much too difficult to put on players' heads.

The Living Conveyor Belt

Play this game in a large space with a rug or clean floor and ask players to remove their shoes. Have players line up side by side and then lie face down with their arms at their sides. Tell the group members they are a living conveyor belt that can carry people along. Ask a player at one end of the conveyor belt to stand up and carefully lay himself face down across the line of people, with his arms stretched out above his head. Then have all the players in the line roll over and over in the direction that this player's arms are pointing. When the player has been rolled along to the other end of the conveyor belt, tell the "rollers" to stop rolling.

It is important that players move gently and that the rollers stay close together. If there are gaps between the rollers, the conveyor belt loses its function. As each player reaches the end of the line, he becomes a roller and the next player takes a turn riding the conveyor belt.

Variations:
- Have players ride the conveyor belt lying on their backs.
- You might have a very large group play this game outside on the grass.

60

Centipede

Tell players that this game comes from Belgium, a country in Western Europe.

Have players line up one behind the other and sit down with their knees bent and their feet flat on the floor. Each player should hold the ankles of the player sitting behind her. Now challenge the line to move forward like a centipede. Invite players to experiment with the fastest ways of moving together. Encourage them to coordinate their movements; they might try chanting "left-right-left-right" and so on. Can the centipede turn to the left and right? Can it move backwards?

Once players have the hang of this game, you might divide the line into two or more teams of equal number and hold centipede races.

Trust Games

Trust is a two-way street. When you put your trust in another person, that person is more likely to trust you in return. In these games, the roles of the one who trusts and the one who is trusted are thrown into relief. For example, one player trusts enough to keep his eyes closed, and the other player takes on the responsibility of keeping him safe.

These trust games contribute to the players' sense of security and their level of confidence in the rest of the group. Each player comes to feel accepted as a group member.

These games are not suitable for groups just beginning to work together. The players should know each other somewhat in order to feel at ease. If these games are introduced too early, they can undermine trust rather than building it.

This type of game is frequently played in pairs. The players should change partners regularly. In the long term, this develops a feeling of mutual responsibility.

61

Running in the Dark

Have players form pairs and hold hands. Ask the partner on the right in each pair to put on a blindfold. Then invite the partner on the left to begin walking slowly, leading his partner beside him. Have pairs gradually increase their speed until they are running. Explain that the point of the game is to discover what it is like to run without being able to see, not to be the fastest runners in the group. Remind the partners without blindfolds to keep their partners safe, and not to move faster than their partners want. Place the emphasis on self-confidence and putting trust in the other person.

After 2 minutes, give a signal for the players to stop. Give partners time to tell each other what they thought of the experience. Have partners switch roles and play again, and then choose new pairs for the next round.

Notes: Have players change partners several times. The role changes have an effect on the freedom of movement. If players are nervous about running blindfolded, you might have them agree on a "slow-down" signal. Maintaining a level of control will help players feel secure.

Silent Contact

♪ **Music:** restful classical music

Have pairs of players spread out around the room, facing each other. Ask players to press both their hands against their partner's hands and close their eyes.

Then put on some restful music. Invite players to move to the music, keeping their hands together. Have them begin by standing in place and making slow, small movements. When the players get used to the game and to each other's movements, you might suggest that they make larger movements and move around the room.

This game is concerned with cooperation. How the couples move is not important.

After a little while, turn the music down as a sign that the partners can gradually stop moving. Let the players then open their eyes again. Give them a little time to talk together.

Variation: Have partners stand face-to-face as above, but keep their palms a few inches apart. One player should close his eyes while the other follows his movements. Then have partners change places. Finally, play the same game with eyes open.

After the game, you might stimulate discussion with questions such as the following: "Did you prefer closing your eyes and leading the movements, or being the follower with open eyes? How is the game different when both partners have their eyes open?"

Robots

Tell players that you are a robot, and invite a volunteer to help you demonstrate. Explain that you have three imaginary control buttons on your shoulders: Pressing the button in the middle makes you walk forward, pressing the button on the left makes you turn left, and pressing the button on the right makes you turn right. Ask the volunteer to press each of your buttons, and move accordingly. Have players form pairs and choose one partner from each pair to be a robot. Explain that the robots should keep their eyes closed.

Tell players that a robot should walk as long as a button is being pressed. If no signal is given, the robot stands still. Have pairs practice this by themselves for a few minutes, and then invite the group to move around together. Challenge the partners who are pressing buttons to insure that there are no collisions. Can they manage that? Then let partners change places.

Exaggeration

Divide the group into teams of five and give each team member a number from one to five. Invite the number ones to move around the room and think of a funny or interesting style of walking.

Have each team observe their own number one as he demonstrates his walking style. Encourage players to notice how number one puts his feet on the floor, the size of his paces, his speed, the way he holds his back and his head, the way he moves his hands, and so on.

Then invite the number twos to get up and walk behind their number one. Ask them to imitate number one's walking style exactly. Gradually invite each of the next three players to join their lines. As the number threes join the line, encourage them to exaggerate the walking style a little, making the movements larger and more obvious. Have the number fours exaggerate the walk even more, and ask the number fives to exaggerate the walk as much as they possibly can. Have the teams continue walking around together.

After number five has joined the line, number one can go to the side of the room and watch the way his team has exaggerated the movements. Then have team members switch numbers and play the game again.

Let Yourself Be Moved

♪ **Music:** peaceful and/or relaxing New Age or classical music

Tell players that in this game, they will find out what it is like to let someone else move them. Have the group form pairs. Ask one partner from each pair to lie on her back, close her eyes, and relax. Tranquil music will help players relax. Then invite the other partner to take her partner's arm gently and slowly move it around. Suggest unhurried movements: The moving partner might lift the arm, lower it, move it to the side, or move the wrist, elbow, and fingers. Encourage the partner lying down to be completely limp and simply allow herself to be moved.

Gradually invite the moving partner to move on to the other arm and both legs. You might have the moving partner sit by her limp partner's head, place two hands on the head, and move it gently back and forth. Then ask partners to change places.

Variations:
- Have players form new pairs. After the game is over, ask whether the change in partners made a difference.
- Play the game as above, but have the limp partner begin the game as a "snail shell." Demonstrate the position for players: Roll up into a ball, with your legs drawn up and your head resting on your knees. Have the moving partner gently unwrap the limp partner until she is lying stretched out but relaxed on the floor.

The Door

Materials: a blindfold

Have players stand in a circle holding hands. Choose one player to stand in the middle; his spot in the circle remains open and becomes the door. Have the players on each side of the door hold one arm at their sides.

Show the player in the center where the door is. Then blindfold him, spin him slowly three times, and have him feel his way to the door. When he has passed through the door, he can take off the blindfold and choose another player to stand in the center.

Variation: Make the game more difficult by having the circle rotate very slowly.

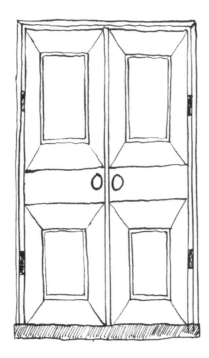

67

Circle of Trust

Make groups of about ten players and have each group stand in a tight circle. Choose one player from each group to take a turn in the center of the circle, standing with feet together, arms folded, and eyes closed. Explain that the player in the middle will fall and the players standing in the circle will catch him. Show players how to stand in catching position: feet slightly apart, knees bent, and hands held out. Urge players to keep the circle tight, with no gaps for the center player to fall through. Invite the center player to rock forward slightly, keeping his feet planted firmly on the ground. Encourage the catchers to support the center player's body lightly with their hands, rather than grabbing it. Have them stand the player upright again. Invite the player in the center to let himself fall a little further if he likes.

End the game gently. The player in the center should first feel that he is firmly back on his feet and only then open his eyes. Then the next player takes a turn.

Expression Games

These games challenge players to express themselves. The games offer a clear structure, but they allow a great amount of freedom within this structure. Players have the opportunity to give shape to their own ideas. These games cannot be "solved" with one correct response; rather, they present a host of possibilities. Players use their creativity to come up with unique solutions to unexpected challenges.

Play these games with groups of players who know each other well. Players need to feel secure in order to express themselves freely. In turn, this free expression will bolster their feelings of self-esteem.

Action Reaction

Explain that you are going to tell a story, and you want players to help. First tell them about a number of elements that will feature in the story. Demonstrate appropriate movements and sounds that correspond to each element. For instance, you might ask players to hop and say "ribbit" every time you mention a frog character or to wave their arms and imitate the sound of surf whenever you mention the sea.

Then tell the story and encourage players to react with the appropriate sound and movement each time you mention the various elements. You can add to the excitement by mentioning elements suddenly or in quick succession. Players will rush to react.

Variations:

- Have players come up with their own movements and sounds to go with the different elements of your story. If necessary, prompt them with questions such as "How could we act like frogs?"
- Have players sit on chairs in a circle. As you tell your story, pause often to ask a player what movement could be made to act out the part of the story you just told. As the story goes on, go around the circle and give each player a turn. Tell players that it is all right to repeat movements made by other players.

Notes: Storytelling is easy to combine with movements. A number of different games are possible. A few general suggestions follow:

- Tell a story featuring all sorts of action moments: This keeps the players active and the story exciting. Don't use too much description.
- Tell a story with a strong plot. Something interesting has to happen. First, briefly present the characters and the setting. Then introduce a problem that the characters must solve. Try to make links between the different elements in this story:

The story problem might be solvable using specific characters' talents—for example, a giant who can be tamed by singing. Thicken the plot with various complications. Continue to work in this way to a climax, at which time the characters solve their problem. Bring the story to a close soon after the climax.

- Tell the story in the present tense; this lends it a feeling of immediacy and inspires the players to move more.
- See the next three games — number 69: "Group Storytelling," number 70: "Relay Story," and number 71: "Tales of Adventure" — for more opportunities to combine storytelling with movement.

Group Storytelling

Invite players to help you make up a story. Explain that everyone will act out the story in movements at the same time. First, tell the beginning of a story: Introduce the characters and setting and present a problem the characters face. Then ask players what happens next. Stand among the children, ready for the next action. Ask questions now and then and use the answers in the story. For instance, consider the following:

"What's that I can see between the branches?"

"A bear!"

"Yes, you're right, it's a bear. What is the bear doing?"

"It's coming toward us!"

"Yes, here it comes, lumbering along and raising its big claws."

Do not be afraid that the storyline will not develop. Acting in the midst of the story will inspire players to come up with creative ideas. Go on building up the story using the children's answers. If necessary, demonstrate a few movements to go along with the narrative.

See the Notes at the end of game number 68: "Action Reaction" for general suggestions on combining storytelling and movement.

Relay Story

Materials: a stick

Tell players that they will take turns making up parts of a story. Tell them that everyone will act out the story in movements at the same time. Hold up a stick and explain that whoever holds the stick is the storyteller. Begin the story by introducing the characters, the setting, and a problem the characters face. Then pass the stick to a player and invite the player to continue the story. The stick is passed from person to person and each player adds to the story in turn. Each player decides for herself how long her part of the story will be. See the Notes at the end of game number 68: "Action Reaction" for general suggestions on combining storytelling and movement.

Variation: Once players have the hang of the game, you might challenge them to play without a stick. Explain that when someone wants to tell the next part of the story, she should simply begin talking. Warn players that when one player stops telling her part of the story, there will be a silence before the next player picks up the story. Tell them that before too long, someone will be inspired to step in. (Do not be tempted to continue the narrative yourself: Have the courage to allow the story to pause for a minute.)

Tales of Adventure

Have players form pairs and hold hands. Explain that each pair will work together to tell the story of an exciting journey. Partners will take turns adding one word to the story. For example:

"I / crawl / through / a / long / tunnel / and / suddenly / see / a / fiery / dragon."

Encourage players to tell the story in the present tense and act it out at the same time.

Explain that this way of storytelling can be frustrating at first. Players may want the story to go in one direction and find that their partners have a different idea altogether. Encourage players to be flexible, listen to each other, and cooperate to build up the story. Point out that telling a story in this way is a real adventure: Players will be constantly surprised by the twists and turns the story makes.

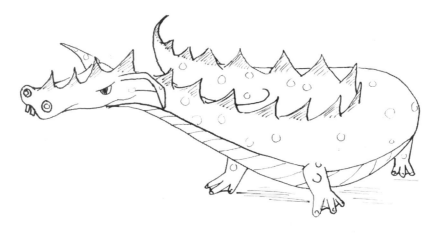

Variation: Pairs act as the hero of their own adventure story. Instead of alternating words, have partners tell longer passages of their stories and switch storytellers at your signal. As above, each pair should hold hands and act out the story in movements as they tell it. The partner who is telling the story should have his eyes open, and the other partner should close her eyes. Encourage players to fill their stories with exciting action: They might sneak through a forest, jump over a stream, or be scared by a lion. Tell them to avoid long descriptions and dialogue. The player whose eyes are open makes sure his partner does not bump into anything. After 2 minutes, have partners change places. After 3.5 minutes, let players know they have 30 seconds left so that they can bring their stories to a close.

Then let the whole group sit down and tell each other briefly about their adventures. Ask which they enjoyed more, having their eyes open or closed. In general, most people seem to enjoy this game best with eyes closed. This seems to give more freedom for fantasy and visualizing the images of the story.

See the Notes at the end of game number 68: "Action Reaction" for general suggestions on combining storytelling and movement.

72

The Magic Ball

Materials: a ball

Sit with players in a circle on the floor. Hold up a ball and tell players that it is magical and can change into different things. Ask how they would hold the ball if it were a big block of ice. (They might shiver and pass the ball along quickly.) Have players pass the "block of ice" around the circle, handling it appropriately. Each time the ball returns to you, change it into something else and encourage players to handle it accordingly. The ball could be a hot potato, a heavy weight, a helium balloon, a sticky honeycomb, a prickly cactus, a sweet smelling rose, and so on. Encourage players to pass the ball around fairly quickly.

Variations:

- Play the game as above, but have players toss the ball back and forth. Encourage players to aim the ball carefully and to be ready to catch it. Once a player has caught the ball, she should handle it appropriately and then toss it to another player. Every so often, call out a new magical identity for the ball.
- Allow older players to decide for themselves what the magic ball is made of. Ask players to show from their movements what kind of ball it is. The player receiving the ball must show through her movements that she knows what kind of ball she has been given. Then she can change it into something else and pass it on. If someone cannot think up a new movement, she can simply pass the ball on in the same way as she received it.

Animal Crackers

Make groups of five to seven players. Ask each group to think up a fantasy animal: for example, an animal with the head of a lion, the wings of an eagle, the front legs of a horse, and the back legs of a lizard. Have each group describe the fantasy animal to another group and challenge the other group to portray the animal with their bodies.

Give the groups time to discuss how they will work together to form their animals. Encourage them to experiment with different strategies. Tell players that every member of the group must be part of the animal and it should be able to move. Then invite the groups to take turns presenting their animals.

Variations:

- Have the groups give each other assignments to make a fantasy machine—a chewing gum machine, perhaps, or a birthday cake machine.
- Allow the players to use all kinds of materials to build their creation: pieces of cloth, paper, chairs, twigs, and so on.

74

Statues

Have players form pairs and spread out around the room. Ask one partner from each pair to turn her back while the other freezes in a "statue" pose. When all the statues are ready, invite the other players to turn around and study their partner's pose for a count of five. Then have the statues sit down in a normal position while the other players try to replicate their partner's pose. Encourage players to tell each other what differences there were between the two statues. Have partners change roles and try again. Then form new pairs and play the game again.

Notes:
- This game can also be played sitting on chairs.
- If the players have difficulty in thinking up poses, give titles to the statues they must create. You might ask them to pose as statues titled "The Dancer," "The Sports Star," "At the Zoo," "The Surprise," "Hard at Work," and so on.

Statue Group

Divide the group into two teams of roughly equal size. Explain that one team will work together to make a group statue. Have the group members sit in a line. The other team will be the audience. Seat them in front of the play area so that everyone can see.

Invite the first player to get up and pose. Have the other players join her one by one. Each subsequent player should choose a pose that fits in with the composition the other players have made. Eventually, a complete statue is built up. The statue might represent a realistic situation, but it could also be abstract.

When the statue is complete, the audience can think up a title. Then have the teams change places.

Variations:

- If players need inspiration at first, give them a title for the statue. For instance: "The Circus," "The Marriage," "In the Playground," or "The Argument." Discourage players from discussing the statue as they take their poses; each player should add her own idea without consulting the others.
- Play a guessing game. Suggest a title to the group about to make the statue. When the statue is complete, challenge the audience to guess what the title was.

Note: Young children and inexperienced players often take up the same pose as the previous player. There is nothing wrong with this. Let it go a couple of times and then suggest that it is fun to choose a different position because variety will make the statue more interesting. Demonstrate a few possibilities so that the players are challenged to add something different to the statue.

Changing Statues

Tell players that in this game, they will be statues in abstract poses. Explain that this means their poses should not portray realistic situations such as driving a car or playing a sport. Demonstrate a few poses that focus on form rather than representation. For example, you might stretch as high as possible or huddle in a ball. Invite a volunteer to pose as the first statue.

Ask the group if anyone can think of a pose that would fit with the first one. This second player goes up and takes his position. Give the group time to look at this new statue formed by two people. Then ask the first player to leave, while the second player maintains his pose.

The second statue now stands alone. Ask a third player to take up a position so that another double statue is formed. Then the second player leaves, the third remains, and a fourth joins him. Continue until everyone has had a turn. The concepts behind the poses will change constantly.

Notes:

- If players are reluctant to volunteer, seat them in a line and have them come forward one by one. More mature players may feel secure enough to come forward when inspired.
- Make sure that when one player leaves a double statue, the other one does not change his pose. A pose often feels very different in isolation, and players must concentrate in order to hold their positions.

Mystery Ball

Materials: several balls of different varieties, such as ping-pong balls, tennis balls, foam rubber balls, rubber balls, footballs, and beach balls; an empty box

Show the group a varied assortment of balls. Display the balls one by one and discuss their names and characteristics with the group. Demonstrate how the balls roll and bounce.

Divide the group in half and have one half of the group watch the others play with the balls. Now and then, encourage players to throw the balls in the air, kick them, bounce them, roll them, and so on. Then let the other half of the group play with the balls. Collect the balls and put them away.

Have players stand in a circle. Invite them to pretend they are playing with the imaginary ball. Stimulate their imaginations with instructions: throw the ball, roll it, bounce it, and so on. After a while, have players pretend to play with another kind of ball. Experiment like this with various kinds of ball.

Variation: After players have pretended to play with all the different types of ball, play a guessing game. Have players sit in a semicircle around an empty box. Pick one player to take an imaginary ball out of the box—the player can decide what kind of ball it is. Ask the player to "play" with the ball. If necessary, give instructions (bounce the ball, throw it, and so on). The other players have to guess what kind of ball it is. The player who guesses correctly can take the next turn.

Note: This game works best with smaller groups.

The Giant's House

Tell players that this game originated in Tanzania, a country in Africa. Divide the group into three or more teams of roughly equal number. Choose one player to stand in the center while all the other players circle around, holding hands and chanting, "Come into the giant's house and say what you can see." Ask the center player to name an object that could be in an imaginary giant's house—point out that she could choose almost anything. Then each team should group together and work to create that object with their bodies. Explain that every player on the team should form a part of the object.

When the teams are finished, have the center player decide which team did the best job; that team wins one point. Then choose a different player to stand in the center for the next round.

Note: This game works best with larger groups.

Games Using Materials

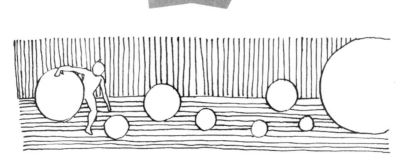

Most movement games do not require materials. Players and enough space are the only ingredients necessary. Still, it can be fun to use objects as the inspiration for movement games.

Each material offers its own possibilities. We have fixed ideas about how to use certain objects: A ball invites players to throw, catch, roll, and bounce it. The challenge is in mastering the technique. Other objects are more open-ended in their potential for movement. Materials like newspaper, cloth, string, and elastic appeal to players' imaginations. They can be used in hundreds of different ways. The players are challenged to explore the material and show their discoveries to each other. It is amazing to see how many possibilities these inexpensive materials have to offer.

79

Fighting Chickens

Materials: a bandana or piece of cloth for each player; string (see note)

Tell players that this game is similar to one from Brazil, a country in South America. Have players pass around bandanas and tuck them into their belts so that most of the bandana hangs free. Demonstrate the fighting chicken stance: Place your left hand on your right shoulder (forming a "wing") and hop on your right foot. Have players practice moving this way for a minute. Explain that the object of the game is for players to steal each other's bandanas and tuck them into their own belts. Even after a player loses her bandana, she can keep trying to steal bandanas. Tell players that they should keep their wings folded and keep hopping on one foot at the same time. The player with the most bandanas at the end of 60 seconds wins. Redistribute the bandanas for the next round.

Note: If any player has no place on her clothing in which to tuck a bandana, loosely tie a piece of string around her waist and tuck the bandana under the string.

Balloon Volleyball

Materials: a balloon and a bandana for every three players; masking tape or chalk for marking the ground

Have players form groups of three. Each member of the trio should face the others and place one hand in the center. Tie the three center hands together with a bandana. Now each trio has a total of four "playing hands": their three outer hands and their one central "hand" tied with the bandana. Use tape or chalk to mark a line dividing the play area into two sections. Put an equal number of groups in each section. Give each trio a balloon and explain that the members must try to make it touch the ground in the other section.

If they succeed, they score one point. The balloon can now be played by another trio. There are a few rules: Trios cannot hold the balloon and walk. They must remain in their own section. It is permitted for one trio to hit a balloon several times in succession.

Play 3 rounds of 3 minutes each.

Variation: Divide the space into more sections. In this case, it is advisable to appoint a scorekeeper for each section.

Boxed In

Materials: chalk or masking tape for marking the ground; a large cardboard box or brown paper grocery bag for every two players

With chalk or masking tape, mark a long wavy trail that loops around to make a complete circuit on the floor. Have players form pairs. Explain that one will begin as the walker and the other as the helper, but they will switch roles often as the game goes on. Give each couple a box or grocery bag; have the walker put the box over his head. The helper leads the walker to a random spot on the wavy line. Tell players that the aim of the game is for the pair to follow the path all the way around to its starting point.

   Point out to the walkers that they can see the line on the floor if they look down. The helpers should put their partners back on track

if they wander off the line. Encourage the helpers to be very quiet. Tell the walkers that they must try not to bump into anyone. They must listen carefully to hear if another player is approaching. If walkers do collide, they should move to the side, take off their boxes, and switch places with their partners. Now the helper becomes the walker.

Variations:

- Have the players wearing boxes make a buzzing sound. Particularly for younger players, this gives a safer feeling; now they can easily hear other players approaching.
- Have the helpers watch from the side of the room and go to their partners only in emergency situations. The walkers follow the line and try to get back to the beginning without bumping into anyone else. Have partners switch places after one round.
- Invite the helpers to take a more active role by giving instructions to the walkers, such as walk forward, walk backwards, turn right, turn left, or stop. Have partners practice on their own before walking on the line.

Sheets and Blankets

Materials: string; clothespins; sheets and/or blankets

This game is a great way to transform a room and give the children a chance to play in a different way. Stretch strings across the room, tying them to window latches, door hinges, cabinet knobs, and so on. Hang sheets and blankets over the strings and affix them with clothespins, creating small "rooms." First give the children time to explore the spaces for themselves. Then take the whole group on a tour of all the rooms.

The hangings give the room a feeling of mystery and invite children to play peek-a-boo and hide-and-seek. The rooms are also very good for fantasy games. Let the children say which rooms they like, which ones they find scary, light, or dark. You can also name the rooms. The addition of dress-up clothes and props makes it even more fun! This environment can make for an entire afternoon of creative play.

The next three games—number 83: "Hat Tag," number 84: "Eek! A Mouse!," and number 85: "The Ghost's Den"—provide opportunities to play more structured games amongst the sheets and blankets.

Hat Tag

Materials: string; clothespins; sheets and/or blankets; a hat

See game number 82: "Sheets and Blankets" for instructions on setting up the playing environment. Hold up a hat and tell players that in this game of tag, the player who is "It" will wear the hat. Whoever is tagged becomes the new "It" and must put on the hat. The sheets and blankets mean that this game is full of surprises: Players may only see who "It" is at the last moment.

Eek! A Mouse!

Materials: string; clothespins; sheets and/or blankets; two hats

See game number 82: "Sheets and Blankets" for instructions on setting up the playing environment. Choose one player to be the cat and another to be the mouse. Have these players wear hats. Explain that the cat must try to catch the mouse. Encourage the other players to help the mouse by hiding her and telling her where the cat is. Players are allowed to talk. When the mouse is caught, she squeaks and all the players gather together. Choose a new cat and mouse for the next round.

The Ghost's Den

Materials: string; clothespins; sheets and/or blankets

See game number 82: "Sheets and Blankets" for instructions on setting up the playing environment. Choose one player to be the ghost and have him hide somewhere in one of the rooms, perhaps under a blanket. He is asleep and snoring. Invite players to run through the rooms and challenge the ghost, singing "Catch me, ghost!"

Suddenly the ghost wakes up, says "boo," and tries to catch the other players. The players who are caught sit together in the ghost's den. One minute after the ghost says "boo," stop the game and have everyone gather in the ghost's den. Count the number of players who were caught and choose a new ghost for the next round.

Roped In

Materials: for every two players, a piece of rope 1-yard long with a knot at each end

♪ **Music:** various selections, both rhythmic and restful

Group players in pairs and give each couple a rope. Ask partners to hold opposite ends of the rope. Have players spread out around the room. Play music and invite pairs to explore what movements they can make while holding the rope between them. Guide them with suggestions such as these:

- Raise your arms and lower them.
- Make the rope dance.
- Take turns stepping over the rope.
- Both of you try to step over the rope at the same time.
- Pull on the rope so that it is stretched tight between you. What movements can you make while keeping the rope taut?

Give time for players to discover what movements they can make with the rope. Play both rhythmic and restful music. Encourage players to keep their movements fluid and make sure they don't let go of the rope.

Variations:

- Allow players to explore movements with the ropes as above. Then mark out a play area that is not too big and have partners sit outside the area. Invite one pair to enter the play area and demonstrate their favorite movement using the rope. Then have another pair join them. Gradually add more and more pairs. There is one rule: Players cannot bump into each other. If players collide, they are out and sit down at the side. In this game, the players must concentrate both on their own movements and on the players around them.

- This time the players should not avoid each other but work with each other. Invite the pairs to weave amongst one other. Encourage partners to hold their rope low enough or high enough so that other players can step over or under it.

Jump Rope

Materials: a length of rope about 15-feet long for each group of three or more players

Hold one end of a length of rope and invite a volunteer to help you turn it in large, easy circles so that the rope rises above players' heads on the way up and almost brushes the floor on the way down. Then invite volunteers to jump over the rope at its low point. Challenge volunteers to stay where they land and jump again when the rope swings around. Once players have the hang of jumping rope, organize them into groups of three or more. Give each group a rope and invite them to take turns jumping and turning the rope. Players should switch roles whenever the jumper makes a mistake.

Variations:

- You might challenge advanced players to try turning or doing other simple tricks as they jump. Groups could create their own sequences of moves and then challenge other groups to repeat them.
- Tell players that people often chant rhymes as they jump rope, such as: "Teddy bear, teddy bear, turn around. Teddy bear, teddy bear, touch the ground." Explain that many chants end with the jumper counting as high as possible before jumping incorrectly. Invite groups to make up their own chants and share them with the other groups.

Chinese Jump Rope

Materials: a Chinese jump rope (or piece of elastic about 4-yards long, knotted to form a loop) for each group of three to five players

This game originated over a thousand years ago in China, and it has long been a popular playground game around the world. Play this on a soft surface (for example, a tumbling mat). Invite two volunteers to help you demonstrate. Have them stand facing each other, about three yards apart, with their legs open. Stretch the Chinese jump rope around their ankles so that it forms a rectangle. Then jump over the rope in a fixed pattern, as you explain to players what you are doing. For example, you might first jump so that both feet land inside the ropes, next jump so that you are straddling the ropes, with one foot on either side, then jump so that your left foot is inside the ropes and your right foot is outside, and finally jump so that your right foot is inside and your left foot is outside. Players might invent any number of patterns.

Explain that when a jumper completes the chosen pattern without making any mistakes, the elastic is raised: first from ankles to knees, and next from knees to thighs. If the jumper makes a mistake, he changes places with one of the "posts" and the series begins again. Have the group agree on a jumping pattern and then form groups of three to five players to try it out.

Variations:
- Invite each group to make up its own jumping pattern. Have groups demonstrate their patterns to the other players.
- Have players explore other movements they can make with the elastic. You might have players walk in pairs with the elastic around their ankles. Encourage them to keep the

elastic taut. Challenge pairs to sit down, lie down, and roll without losing the elastic. Once they have mastered this, they might try it with the elastic around their knees or waists or tucked under their armpits.

- Invite groups of three or four to explore moving together, bound by the elastic. Groups might try some of the same exercises suggested for pairs above. Play quiet music to help players concentrate. Then let the groups demonstrate their best discoveries to the others.

Bench Races

Materials: two or more long, free-standing benches without backrests

Young children often enjoy this simple game because everyone is moving all the time. Set two benches parallel to each other, with plenty of space between them. Divide the group into two teams of equal numbers, one team for each bench. Have players sit astride the benches, one behind the other. Ideally, there should be enough players to cover the whole length of each bench. Tell all the players to slide forward, and invite the player in front to jump up, run around to the back of the bench, and sit down in the newly created space there. Have players slide forward again and have the next player run around to the back, and so on. Once players have the hang of this, ask the teams to race to see who can finish with the first player back in her original spot at the front of the bench.

Variation: Line up two or more benches end to end and have a large group play the game as a race against time. Time the group with a stopwatch and give it a few chances to beat its own record.

Gate Ball

Materials: a ball

Have players stand in a large circle with their legs spread out so that their feet touch those of their neighbors and there are no open spaces. Display a ball and tell players that they must keep the ball from going between their legs (the "gate"). Explain that players can only use their hands to move the ball; they should not kick the ball or bring their knees together. Hand the ball to a player and invite him to begin the game by trying to throw or roll the ball between another player's legs. That player should try to catch or block the ball and send it toward the legs of another player, and so on.

If the ball goes through a gate, that player is out and leaves the circle. You might have players who are out watch the game or wait in line: When four players are out, the first can join in again.

Variation: With a large group, you might choose to form two circles, each with its own ball, and have two games going simultaneously. When players are called out of one game, they can join the other circle. This way everyone continues to play.

Catch-Up Ball

Materials: two balls (optional: two or more balls of one color and two or more balls of another color)

Have players stand in a circle and count off alternately one and two. Explain that the ones are a team and the twos are another team. Players should remain in their places in the circles. Give a ball to a player from team one. Tell her to throw the ball to her nearest teammate on the left (in other words, to the player two spaces over to the left). Have the number ones continue passing the ball around the circle in a clockwise direction until it returns to the starting point. Then give the ball to a player from team two and have team two practice passing the ball around the circle in the same way. Encourage players to remember who their nearest teammates are.

Then give one ball to a player from team one and another ball to a player from team two standing at the opposite side of the circle. Explain that each team should pass the ball clockwise around the circle as fast as possible. If a player drops the ball, she should pick it up and keep playing. Point out that if one team passes the ball faster than the other team, its ball will begin to catch up to the other team's ball. Tell players that if one team's ball passes the other team's ball, the passing team wins a point. Then the game stops and the balls begin again at opposite sides of the circle for the next round. Invite players to begin the game.

Variation: In a large group the game can be played using two or three balls for each team. Give the teams balls of different colors so that they are easy to distinguish. Any ball that is overtaken is removed from the game. The team that keeps its final ball going longest is the winner.

The Atlas Game

Materials: "Earth ball" (a large ball at least 1 yard in diameter) or a very large balloon if the players are small children

Place the "Earth ball" in the center of the group. Have players gather around the ball as closely as possible. Then invite them to lift the ball together, slowly and carefully. Have players hold the ball above their heads with outstretched arms.

Now, encourage the whole group to try to walk together without dropping the ball. Challenge them to walk faster. You might have players try the following activities:

- Spin the ball in various directions.
- Stand on tiptoes, then squat down to the ground.
- Lie down together without letting the ball drop. (Point out that, in order to do this, players must turn their hands around while still supporting the ball. This is a challenge!)
- Move the ball through an obstacle course. (Have the group carry the ball over, under, through, and between various obstacles, such as playground equipment.)

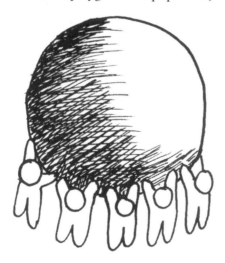

Globe-Ball Circle

Materials: "Earth ball" (a large ball with a diameter of at least 1 yard)

Have players sit in a large circle on the floor. Demonstrate the proper position for this game: Sit with your hands planted on the ground behind you and your legs stretched out in front of you. Place the ball in the circle and explain that players should use only their feet to move it. Encourage them to pass the ball to one another so that everyone has the ball at least once.

Variations:

- Have players lie in a large circle on their stomachs with their hands towards the center. In this version, players must use their hands to pass the ball.
- Have players form a small circle this time and lie on their backs with their hands and feet in the air. Challenge them to pass the ball around the circle on their hands and feet without letting it fall to the ground. Cooperation is very important in this game.

Stick Work

Materials: a stick 1 yard in length for every two players

Have players form pairs and give each pair a stick. Partners should stand facing each other in two long lines. Tell players that they will work together to hold up the stick, but they should not grasp it: Partners must support the stick between them by each pressing the palm of one hand against one end of the stick. Invite a volunteer to help you demonstrate. Give pairs a chance to practice, and then ask them to hold their sticks up high, forming a tunnel. Challenge the pair at the front of the line to pass through the tunnel, keeping their stick supported between them the whole time. When they reach the end of the tunnel, the pair can raise their stick again and join the back of the line. Have the next pair pass through the tunnel, and so on until everyone has had a turn. If partners drop their stick, they should pick it up again and keep going.

Variations:

- Have every other pair hold their sticks down low, so that the sticks alternate high and low. Now the pair moving down the row must go through an obstacle course, weaving over and under the sticks.
- You may wish to adapt the game for younger children by allowing them to grasp the sticks. For older players, you can make the game more challenging by having them press the sticks between their thumbs.

Obstacle Kickball

Materials: tennis balls or other balls of similar size; boxes, road cones, or other objects for making obstacles; tape or chalk for marking the ground; magic markers for marking the balls

Display the balls and tell players that they are going to design an obstacle course and kick these balls through it. Help players use boxes, cones, and other common objects to create obstacles for the balls to go around, tunnels for them to go through, and perhaps ramps for them to roll up and over. Have players mark the correct route through the course using tape or chalk. Then have them mark the starting and finish lines.

Organize players into roughly equal teams of two to six players each. Give each team a ball and have them color it with a marker so that it is easy to distinguish from the other teams' balls. Have each team choose one member who will kick the ball first. Tell players that after the first kick, team members should work together to move their ball through the course. Explain that each team member can kick the ball only twice in a row before giving another team member a chance. Of course, the balls must follow the correct route through the course, passing around, over, or through every obstacle. Have teams line up at the starting line; then give the signal for the first player on each team to kick the ball. The team whose ball crosses the finish line first wins.

Tell players that a game similar to this one is played by Tarahumara Indians of Mexico. Explain that there's one big difference: They traditionally play on huge outdoor courses that may be as long as 40 miles!

Music and Movement Games

Many of the games in this book have used background music to relax players or to encourage them to move more vigorously. In the games that follow, music and sound do not merely influence the atmosphere; they play an essential role.

The Driving Dance

Materials: chairs; blackboard

♪ **Music:** rhythmic music in 4/4 time (e.g., reggae or boogie-woogie)

This game is designed to suit a classroom setting. Tell players that they will work together to make up a group dance that can be done sitting on chairs. Ask the players how people move when they drive cars. Have volunteers demonstrate the various movements. For each one, write a key word or phrase on the blackboard. For instance:

- starting (players might turn the key in the ignition and press the accelerator with their right foot)
- backing up (players might shift the gears with their right hand and look over their right shoulder)
- turning right (players might rotate an imaginary steering wheel clockwise with both hands)

Continue until you have a list of several actions. Explain that players will use these movements as the different steps of a dance. Each movement should be done to the count of eight. Have players practice the movements one after the other. Encourage players to look at the board as little as possible.

When the players are comfortable with the movements, add the music. First play a short fragment so that players hear the rhythm, then give a signal for everyone to begin the driving dance.

Left Foot, Right Foot

♪ **Music:** rhythmic music, such as marching band music

Tell players that this game is played in Liberia, a country in Africa. Play music and have everyone stand in a circle and clap in time. To demonstrate the game, play the role of "It" for the first round. Stand in the center of the circle and, to the rhythm of the clapping, hop toward a player until you are standing in front of him. Still in rhythm, lift one leg with bent knee and toe pointing down. Tell the player to lift the same leg you did (i.e., the left leg if you lifted the left, the right leg if you lifted the right).

Explain that, once play really begins, the player "It" chooses will have to lift his leg at exactly the same time "It" does. If the player lifts the wrong leg, or if he moves slower than the rhythm of the clapping, he will take the place of "It" in the center for the next round. Have the player who helped you demonstrate take the first turn as "It."

Picture the Sound

Materials: musical instruments and/or other objects for making sound effects

This is a short game to get the group moving and strengthen the concentration. Tell players that in this game, the motions they make should be inspired by the sounds they hear. Play a beat on a drum or other rhythm instrument and have players move around the room to the rhythm. When the sound stops, everyone should freeze. Then play a different rhythm on a different instrument and have players move again.

Encourage players to think about the different sounds and move in ways that feel right with the sounds they hear. For example, a tambourine might inspire a smooth, slithering motion, while a drum might invite heavy stomping. You don't have to limit yourself to musical instruments for this game: Objects such as whistles, pans, paper, or a sheet of metal can produce a variety of interesting sound effects. This game is a good warm-up exercise for the expression games.

Blow Up
the Balloon

In this game, movement is inspired by sound effects the players make themselves. Have the group stand in a large circle. Choose five players to form a smaller circle in the middle. Ask them to hold hands and squat down close to each other. Explain that these players are a balloon, and the group can inflate the balloon by making blowing noises.

As the outside players make blowing noises, encourage the center players to imitate a balloon inflating. They should slowly rise and step backwards, making their circle bigger and bigger. Point out that the balloon is getting too full of air, and soon it will pop. When the inner circle can expand no longer and the players have to part hands, the outside players should clap once loudly to represent the pop and then make the sounds of a balloon deflating. Encourage the balloon players to "explode" away from each other out to the edges of the room. Then have them join the outer circle and choose five new players to form a balloon for the next round.

Musical Robots

Materials: simple musical instruments (rhythm instruments, kazoos, and so on)

Tell players that in this game they will pretend to be sound-activated robots. Different sounds will cause the robots to move in different ways. Explain that, for example, a beat on the drum might make a robot take a step forward, while a shake of the tambourine might make the robot turn its head.

Divide the group into pairs and provide them with lots of different musical instruments. Have partners work together to decide on five different sound signals and the motions they will cause. Point out to the players that they may be able to make a variety of sounds on a single instrument. Tell them they can also decide to use their voices to create some of the signals. Give them time to explore different sounds and practice the movements. Partners should take turns being the robot and the sound controller.

Finally, have each pair present a demonstration to the group. Partners can decide for themselves who will play which part. Challenge spectators to guess which sound produces each movement.

Don't
Space Out

♪ **Music:** up-tempo piano music

Divide the group in half and have the two groups join hands to form two circles, one inside the other. The players in the outer circle should be spaced about an arm's length apart; the players in the inner circle should move closer together to make their circle smaller. Tell the group that the players in each circle should be evenly spaced. Have players drop their hands and turn to the right. Play music and have both circles begin to move in time to the music, making sure that the distances between players remain equal.

When players have the hang of this, call out the names of two players, one from each group, who should switch circles. They should join their new circles in the spots closest to them, rather than find each other's original spaces. Encourage players to adjust to the change so that the distances between the players in each circle equalize. Repeat this every so often. Once the group is working together well, you can increase the frequency with which the players change over.

Variations:

- Increase the level of difficulty by having the circles move in opposite directions. The players now have to react very quickly, turn around, and move in a different direction with the new circle.
- Add to the challenge by playing faster music.

The Games Arranged
According to Age Groups

Young Children

Older Children

69. Group Storytelling
70. Relay Story
71. Tales of Adventure
72. The Magic Ball
73. Animal Crackers
75. Statue Group
76. Changing Statues
77. Mystery Ball
78. The Giant's House
79. Fighting Chickens
80. Balloon Volleyball
81. Boxed In
87. Jump Rope
88. Chinese Jump Rope
91. Catch-Up Ball
95. Obstacle Kickball
96. The Driving Dance
97. Left Foot, Right Foot
99. Blow Up the Balloon
100. Musical Robots
101. Don't Space Out

Adolescents (Grades 6-8)

1. Lobster Soup
2. Code Tag
3. Liberation Tag
4. Cross-Tag
5. I Dare You
7. Line Tag
8. Tease the Wolf
9. Fishing Nets
10. The Hungry Shark
11. Back-Hand Tag
12. Boundary Tag
16. Mirror Game
19. Forest Tag
20. Night Prowlers
27. Make the Right Move
34. Bump Jump
41. Street and Avenues
42. The Empty Chair
43. Too Late, Neighbor
44. Group Seven
48. Name Tag
49. In a Knot
51. Push Me, Pull You
58. Hats Off to Teamwork!
59. The Living Conveyor Belt
61. Running in the Dark
63. Robots
70. Relay Story
73. Animal Crackers

75. Statue Group
76. Changing Statues
79. Fighting Chickens
80. Balloon Volleyball
87. Jump Rope
88. Chinese Jump Rope
91. Catch-Up Ball
95. Obstacle Kickball
96. The Driving Dance
100. Musical Robots

Teenagers (Grades 9-12)

3. Liberation Tag
4. Cross-Tag
11. Back-Hand Tag
12. Boundary Tag
16. Mirror Game
34. Bump Jump
43. Too Late, Neighbor
44. Group Seven
49. In a Knot
51. Push Me, Pull You
58. Hats Off to Teamwork!
59. The Living Conveyor Belt
61. Running in the Dark
62. Silent Contact
65. Let Yourself Be Moved
67. Circle of Trust
70. Relay Story
75. Statue Group
76. Changing Statues
79. Fighting Chickens
91. Catch-Up Ball
95. Obstacle Kickball
96. The Driving Dance

All Ages

6. Chase the Dragon's Tail
18. Slow Motion
21. Freezing and Thawing
23. Moving Joints
50. Don't Drop the Ball
55. Fancy Footwork
74. Statues
86. Roped In
90. Gate Ball
92. The Atlas Game
93. Globe-Ball Circle
94. Stick Work
98. Picture the Sound

The SmartFun activity books encourage imagination, social interaction, and self-expression in children. Games are organized by the skills they develop and marked for appropriate age levels, times of play, and group size. Most games are noncompetitive and require no special skills or training. The series is widely used in homes, schools, day-care centers, clubs, and summer camps.

101 MUSIC GAMES FOR CHILDREN: Fun and Learning with Rhythm and Song by Jerry Storms

All you need to play these 101 music games are music tapes or CDs and simple instruments, many of which kids can have fun making from common household items. Many games are especially good for large group settings, such as birthday parties and day-care. Others are easily adapted to meet classroom needs. No musical knowledge is required.

Over 200,000 copies sold in 11 languages worldwide

160 pages ... 30 illus. ... Paperback $12.95 ... Spiral bound $17.95

101 MORE MUSIC GAMES FOR CHILDREN: New Fun and Learning with Rhythm and Song by Jerry Storms

This action-packed compendium offers ingenious song and dance activities from a variety of cultures. These help children enjoy themselves while developing a love for music. Besides listening, concentration, and expression games, this book includes rhythm games, dance and movement games, relaxation games, card and board games, and musical projects.

192 pages ... 72 illus. ... Paperback $12.95 ... Spiral bound $17.95

101 DANCE GAMES FOR CHILDREN: Fun and Creativity with Movement by Paul Rooyackers

The games in this book combine movement and play in ways that encourage children to interact and express how they feel in creative fantasies and without words. They are organized into meeting and greeting games, cooperation games, story dances, party dances, "musical puzzles," dances with props, and more. No dance training or athletic skills are required.

160 pages ... 30 illus. ... Paperback $12.95 ... Spiral bound $17.95

For more information visit www.hunterhouse.com

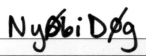

101 DRAMA GAMES FOR CHILDREN: Fun and Learning with Acting and Make-Believe *by* Paul Rooyackers

These noncompetitive games include introduction games, sensory games, pantomime games, story games, sound games, games with masks, games with costumes, and many more. The "play-ful" ideas in *101 Drama Games for Children* help to develop creativity and self-esteem, improvisation, communication, and trust.

160 pages ... 30 illus. ... Paperback $12.95 ... Spiral bound $17.95

UPCOMING BOOKS IN THIS SERIES...

101 MOVEMENT GAMES FOR CHILDREN: Fun and Learning with Playful Moving *by* Huberta Wiertsema
August 2002

These games include variations on old favorites such as "Duck, Duck, Goose" as well as new games such as "Mirroring," "Equal Pacing," and "Moving Joints."

101 MORE DRAMA GAMES FOR CHILDREN: New Fun and Learning with Acting and Make-Believe
by Paul Rooyackers   *August 2002*

Includes improvisational games that encourage total involvement and cooperation from participants and offer a wealth of possibilities for play sessions.

101 MORE DANCE GAMES FOR CHILDREN: New Fun and Creativity with Movement
by Paul Rooyackers   *November 2002*

Introductory Games, Animal Dance Games, Character Dance Games, Street Dance Games, Dance a Story, Dancing with Props, and Dance Notations.

YOGA GAMES FOR CHILDREN: Fun and Fitness with Postures, Movements and Breath
by Danielle Bersma and Marjoke Visscher   *November 2002*

A playful introduction to yoga for children ages 6–12. The games help young people develop body awareness, physical strength, and flexibility. The 54 exercises are variations on traditional yoga exercises, adjusted for children.

All books $12.95 paperback, $17.95 spiral bound

All prices subject to change